WITHDRAWN

HARVARD LIBRARY

WITHDRAWN

The Press and Vatican II

THE PRESS AND VATICAN II

Edward L. Heston, C.S.C.

University of Notre Dame Press
Notre Dame – London

Copyright © 1967 by

University of Notre Dame Press

Library of Congress Catalog Card No. 66-14630

Manufactured in the United States of America

by NAPCO Inc.

FOREWORD

POPE PAUL VI, addressing journalists a few days before the close of the Ecumenical Council, Vatican II, spoke of the "considerable importance" of the role of the press in the historic four-year effort at *aggiornamento*—"updating" of the church.

"If the church has felt," he said, "as never before in its two-thousand-year history, so many millions of men interested in the meeting of bishops of the entire world, it is without any doubt, dear sirs, to you that this is owed very largely."

Another distinguished Council participant, less exalted, therefore less restrained than the Supreme Pontiff, has asserted that world public opinion, mobilized by the press, played a "decisive role" in encouraging the successful, progressive drive of the Council majority.

These views indicate why it is useful and important to trace the evolution of Council press policy from the original naive assumption that 2500 prelates could meet in privacy and virtual secrecy for parts of four years to reshape the Church of half a billion people to the healthy realization that *aggiornamento* in camera is no *aggiornamento* at all.

And the man best equipped to tell of it, at least from the standpoint of the English-language press, is the author of this volume, Father Edward L. Heston, C.S.C. As head of the American Bishops' Press Panel at the first session in 1962 and as English-language briefing officer at the three succeeding sessions, he played a role in the development of satisfactory press arrangements much larger than that suggested by the two or three modest, third-person references to himself in his book.

He does not report, for example, that it was he who first broke through the deadening limitations of the official bulletin system. On his first day as English-language briefing officer in 1963, he dutifully read his translation of the official Italian bulletin to an apathetic press corps. From that meeting he went directly to the American prelate in charge of the U.S. Bishops' Press Panel and made his declaration of independence, demanding support for presentation of his own English-language report on the day's Council proceedings. This produced rumblings from "higher authority" from time to time when the English bulletin reported in detail some of the more unorthodox, hence newsworthy, opinions voiced in the aula. But with support from his immediate superiors, Father Heston's policy of candor continued.

For these labors, Father Heston won the respect of the several hundred journalists to whom he ministered. As a warm, kindly, Christian man and priest, he also won their affection.

ROBERT C. DOTY
Rome Correspondent,
The New York Times

November 27, 1965

PREFACE

IT is only natural that the end of the Second Ecumenical Vatican Council would result in the publication of more than a few volumes. In fact, the Sessions prior to the final one were responsible for many books, not all of equal value as aids in understanding adequately the sweeping aims and the new spirit of Vatican II. Even so, some may wonder why another volume is being added to the many already published.

This book undertakes to tell a story that could easily be lost sight of in the overall history of the Council but which nonetheless has a value and an interest all its own. Arrangements for the press covering the Council, although they eventually turned out to the general satisfaction of all interested parties, did not fall ready-made from heaven. It took time to work out all the difficulties, and the story of the process has a particular interest even for the general public. The books that undertake to tell the Council story in terms of debates and conflicts will not, perhaps, stop to wonder just how the elements of this story were actually brought before the public.

As far as the Council and the press were concerned, much more was involved than actually met the eye of the casual observer or even of the more expert participant. The ultimate news stories on front pages throughout the world were the result of an evolution of policy that was not always painless. The story told here shows how mutual understanding of problems and a generous measure of good will can result in satisfactory solutions that serve the best interests of a common cause.

This little book is not in any way official. From his vantage point in the English-language press office of the Council the author was well placed to see at close range the problems confronting the press, as well as their impact on the daily image of the Council before the world. Nevertheless, his telling of the "press story" of the Second Ecumenical Vatican Council is exclusively on his own authority, not that of the Council Press Office.

A final word. As mentioned above, many books in various languages have undertaken to acquaint the world with the story of the Council's more than three years of difficult but fruitful work. Therefore this present volume ignores the day-to-day chronology of the Council, its discussions, its speakers, the main points debated on the floor, and so forth. Its sole purpose is to show how Vatican II gradually faced up to its press problem, unique in conciliar history, and worked out a satisfactory solution.

A special word of appreciation is owed to two members of the working Council press corps who read the manuscript and offered many valuable suggestions that have found their way into the text: Mrs. Anna Brady, Rome correspondent for *The Long Island Catholic,* and Mr. Weldon Wallace, correspondent for the *Baltimore Sun.* The author is deeply indebted to both.

Cordial thanks also go to Mr. Robert C. Doty, Rome correspondent of *The New York Times,* for adding his personal prestige and that of his paper to this modest volume.

For indispensable secretarial assistance in the various stages of the preparation of the manuscript, the author dutifully thanks Brother James Willson, C.S.C., of the Eastern Priests' Province of the Congregation of Holy Cross.

> EDWARD L. HESTON, C.S.C.
> English-language Press Officer
> II Ecumenical Vatican Council

ROME, December 8, 1965

CONTENTS

    Foreword   5

    Preface   9

    List of Illustrations   14

1   Vatican II: First Council with a Press Problem   17

2   Early Organization of the Council Press Office   25

3   A Press Officer's Day   33

4   The United States Bishops' Press Panel   39

5   Session I   47

6   Session II   55

7   Session III   81

8   Session IV   87

    Conclusion   97

    Appendix   103

    Address of Pope Paul VI to Council Press Corps   123

    Address of Pope John XXIII to Council Press Corps   129

ILLUSTRATIONS

Pope John XXIII addressing newsmen   69

Pope John with the Papal Chamberlain and Master of Pontifical Ceremonies   69

Cartoon satirizing Session I press policy   70

Organizing committee for U.S. Bishops' Press Panel   71

Briefing of English-language journalists   72

Father Heston briefing journalists   73

Pope Paul VI addressing press corps   74, 75

Staff of the Council Press Office   74

Basilica, showing position of Press Officers   75

Briefing by members of U.S. Bishops' Press Panel   76

Episcopal Commission meeting with Press Officers   77

Members of U.S. Bishops' Press Panel, Session III   78

Msgr. Fausto Vallainc chatting with newsmen   79

Cardinal Alfrink addressing journalists   80

THE PRESS AND VATICAN II

1

VATICAN II
FIRST COUNCIL WITH A PRESS PROBLEM

AMONG many other "firsts" the Second Ecumenical Vatican Council was the first in the centuries-old history of the Roman Catholic Church to have to deal with a world press daily on a broad scale. Councils up to and including the Council of Trent (1545–1563) were not confronted with any press problem. They did not even attempt to keep the public informed of their discussions and decisions on a day-to-day basis. In fact, there were no means for rapid diffusion of news. On one occasion the papal legates at Trent were well pleased when they could dispatch a swift courier to Rome with reasonable assurance that their urgent request for instructions would reach the Vatican within five or six days. There was little general interest in the news of the Council or its decrees until they were promulgated in papal pronouncements and posted at church doors for those who could read or, for professors and research scholars, until the later appearance of imposing and ponderous volumes of conciliar acts.

When Vatican Council I convened December 8, 1869, under the presidency of Pope Pius IX, the world situation was somewhat different. Telegraph and cable service were in their infancy, but nothing like long-distance, let alone intercontinental, telephone service was available. Postal service was slow and left much to be desired. But, most of all, the general pace of life had not yet reached the impatient tempo of the twentieth century.

Some correspondents covering Vatican Council I were less day-to-day reporters than long-range commentators on a story that, to tell the truth, was not particularly rich in public interest. In 1869 the Roman Catholic Church was hardly at the center of world attention. The decades of revolution through which Europe had been passing had threatened a Church quite out of contact with the feel of the times. Circumstances were forcing churchmen to direct their gaze more to the inside and self-preservation than to the outside and influence on the world and the men living in it. The belief that "the gates of hell shall not prevail" had brought an undue sense of security and a lessened sense of responsibility for the millions throughout the world. Such an attitude, although inspired by the best motives and valid theological considerations necessarily inspired an attitude of open antipathy or cold disinterest by most observers. Also, the Roman Catholic Church was regarded as more or less synonymous with the Papal States, and most people paid no more attention to the Papal States than to any other tiny principality in Europe. Any interest aroused was definitely hostile. For instance, on the eve of the opening of Vatican I, Naples was host to an assembly that called itself "The Anti-Council of Free-Thinkers." Its avowed aim was to discredit the Council and all it stood for.

These sketchy notes provide some explanation of why the world was not terribly interested in Vatican I as "world news," insofar as anything like world news was possible at the time. The "closed corporation" mentality mentioned had its unavoidable repercussions on public relations. The few correspondents on hand were given little or no cooperation by officials. Consequently, it was inevitable that they should go to unofficial sources, even professional tipsters, to get information. Although many of the Council Fathers at Vatican I saw nothing anomalous in this regrettable situation, others, particularly in the Anglo-Saxon group, considered the official attitude a genuine source of danger. In a letter written during the Council, Doctor Ullathorne, Bishop of Birmingham, England, describes the situation graphically. Dom Christopher Butler, O.S.B., Abbot of Downside, sums up the comments in Doctor Ullathorne's letters in *The Vatican Council* (1869–1870) published in 1962, a shortened study based on his earlier volume of the same title.

The special correspondents of the great newspapers naturally chafed before the thick veil of secrecy that concealed all that was going on in the Council. They were for the most part altogether hostile, and their reports sought to damage the Council in every possible way. Prominent among them was the special correspondent sent out by the *Times*. In excuse for him must be allowed his own statement that "he was known to have no acquaintance with the Italian language and people" and was compelled to rely on the English gossip he could pick up.

Doctor Ullathorne himself wrote on December 23, 1869:

The *Times* correspondent has entertained the world with the most astounding decisions, dissensions and confusion in the Council. President stopped bishops by his bell, 130 bishops walked out of the Council in disgust, and all sorts of protests have been made against oppression of our liberty of speech and action: the fact being that not a bishop has yet opened his mouth except in prayer and singing and uttering certain formularies. The *Times* has much to say about a certain Bull that has angered the bishops until the Pope durst not publish it in the Session, the fact being that this so-called Bull is the method of proceeding distributed at the pre-Synodal Assembly in the Sistine Chapel, containing the ordinary rules of a General Council. The correspondent has even got a glimpse of it, and quoted from it, as an astute obtaining of secret information—the document being posted all the while on the walls of the city. . . . Well did I advise the Faithful in the pastoral to trust nothing but authentic documents.

Despite the policy of withholding official news of Council doings, Doctor Ullathorne was sanguine enough to hope that "the next Council will allow free access to the world press." In this he shared the view expressed in the Council by Archbishop Darboy of Paris—who was to fall before a Commune firing squad in 1871—when he voiced the fear that the Council might not measure up to its task "in the judgment of those who make up the queen of the world, public opinion."

The feeling at the time, reflected in Dom Butler's work (p. 486), was that the interests of the Council would have been much better served by a greater spirit of openness, by more publicity. Such a policy, which Dom Butler would have extended even to the presence of press representatives at the General Congregations, would have forestalled the publication of inaccurate and patently unobjective accounts that were sometimes reproduced extensively in the world press. Writing back in 1930, Dom Butler was of the opinion that the perfect solution would have been the publication of a *weekly* bulletin with a resumé of the discussions and decisions of the Council. On November 7, 1965, in an address on social communications in the world today at La Cittadella Cristiana in Assisi, Cardinal Franziskus Koenig, Archbishop of Vienna, in perfect agreement with Dom Butler, declared that the policy of secrecy imposed during Vatican I had done the Council more harm than good. It aroused distrust and suspicion. A press hostile to the Church had full freedom to print what it pleased, whereas the bishops, bound by the strict secrecy of the Council, were prevented from offering effective counter measures to the erroneous reports so easily put into circulation.

No such thing as a press office had even been contemplated for Vatican I. Any news that filtered out came from private sources. Father D'Alzon, founder of the Congregation of the Assumptionists, feeling the need for enlightening the public, undertook on his own initiative to provide unofficial information. With laudable zeal and almost incredible perseverance, Father D'Alzon wrote over four hundred letters during the ten months that Vatican I was in session. When we recall how the people of that generation were given to lengthy epistles like those of Doctor Ullathorne, and that they did all their writing in longhand, we get some idea of the great service that Father D'Alzon rendered to those outside the Council.

Not quite a hundred years were to pass before Vatican II was announced by Pope John XXIII in his dramatic speech in the Basilica of St. Paul on January 25, 1959, Feast of the Conversion of the Apostle of the Nations. The place of the Church in the world had changed radically since 1869. The great modern popes from Leo XIII through Pius XII had earned the respect of the entire world. John XXIII had a prestige and affection rarely equalled in the annals of the papacy. There was room for improvement in many ways, but the overall situation was certainly encouraging.

Vatican II was convoked by Pope John XXIII in circumstances ideal for the spread of its message. What is more important, the world was genuinely interested in the Council and in its message. The latest advances in telegraph, cable, international and intercontinental telephone services had been supplemented by sophisticated progress in radio and television. At the beginning transoceanic jet plane service could insure in many parts of the world evening television screening of scenes in the Council hall that very morning. Before the Council was very old, satellites expedited communications still more. No Council in Church history had such opportunities for public relations.

2

**EARLY ORGANIZATION OF THE
COUNCIL PRESS OFFICE**

IN the light of official policy during Vatican I, there was much speculation as to what consideration the press could expect in Vatican II. Any misgivings were at least partially allayed when, on October 30, 1960, at a conference for some two hundred representatives of the press, Cardinal Domenico Tardini, Vatican Secretary of State and the prelate directly charged with the preparatory phase of the Council, assured the assembled journalists that studies were under way to determine how news of the Council preparations and of its sessions could be made available to the world press. This first announcement was followed on December 3, 1960, by a further statement by Archbishop Pericle Felici, Secretary General of the Council, to a group of Italian Catholic journalists assembled in convention at the *Domus Mariae* in Rome. The Archbishop stated that there would definitely be a press office for the Council.

On April 18, 1961, headquarters were set up in Via dei Serristori 12, near St. Peter's. Nothing was really organized, and, to repeat the words of the Secretary, the press office was "more interested in getting news than in giving it out." On June 20, 1961, Pope John XXIII, addressing the assembled Members and Consultors of the Council's Preparatory Commissions, praised the sincere desire of most journalists to secure precise Council news, although he added the gently chiding remark that they were sometimes "a bit impatient" in their desire to gather information. Nevertheless, he thanked them for their interest and pointed out that an Ecumenical Council is by its nature different from any national or international gathering.

The diligence of the press thus far was most laudable since it had had very little to go on. Accounts of the meetings of the Central Preparatory Commission appeared in the Vatican newspaper *L'Osservatore Romano,* which reprinted the Press Office bulletins. There were ninety-seven of these, which in Italian run to some three hundred mimeographed pages. Nevertheless, the content could hardly be classified as news because there was no real meaty information.

Later that year, on October 25, 1961, Pope John XXIII received the press corps of Rome in special audience. He informed them that the Council Press Office was gradually taking shape. In this audience the Pope remarked that he was fully aware of the valuable contribution the press could make in publicizing the work of the Council.

About this time a special assistant was appointed to Archbishop Felici. This was Monsignor Fausto Val-

Early Organization of the Council Press Office

lainc, from the diocese of Aosta, Italy, who had been for some years Ecclesiastical Consultant to the Italian Catholic Press Union, which serves as the press office for the national headquarters of Italian Catholic Action. Three weeks later, on November 17, 1961, in an address at the end of the second meeting of the Council's Central Preparatory Commission, Pope John again spoke of the role of the press: "We are also happy because the men of our time, and in particular the journalists, have followed your work with attention and with a diligence worthy of praise." On May 12, 1962, when closing the discussions of the sixth meeting of the Central Preparatory Commission, Pope John announced that a more substantial organization of the Press Office was being worked out "to assure that public opinion will be properly informed."

As then organized the Council Press Office depended directly on the Secretary General of the Council, Archbishop Pericle Felici. To meet the needs of the international press corps, seven language sections were established under Monsignor Vallainc, the Press Office secretary. The following priests were in charge of the individual offices:

English — Monsignor James Tucek, of Dallas, Texas, director of the NCWC news bureau in Rome

French — Father François Bernard, A.A., assistant editor of *La Croix,* French Catholic daily

German	Monsignor Gerhard Fittkau, professor of ecclesiology at the seminary of Essen, Germany and counsellor of the German National Radio
Italian	Father Francesco Farusi, S.J., of Vatican Radio
Polish	Father Stefan Wesoly, chaplain for Polish emigrants in Italy;
Portuguese	Father Paolo Almeida, S.J., of Vatican Radio
Spanish	Father Cipriano Calderon, vice rector of the Pontifical Spanish College and Rome correspondent for the Spanish Catholic press.

Father Mounged Hachem, a priest of the Oriental Maronite rite, prepared news bulletins in Arabic, although at that time not daily.

Before the opening of the Council, the job of the Press Office was largely to provide background information for the journalists, most of whom were understandably short on the historical and theological knowledge required. The Press Office had prepared a translation in four languages—English, French, German, and Spanish—of four documents of general interest: "The Preparation of the Council"; "Structure and Functioning of the Preparatory Commissions"; "Glossary of Council Terms"; "Explanation of Some Topics to be Discussed in the Council." During this period installation of modern communications equipment was under way to assure the most rapid transmission of news and photos. The Press Office also provided 112 other documentary releases.

In May, 1962, Pope John XXIII approved the organization of special Press Office headquarters to serve the journalists coming to the Council. The pressroom, in Via della Conciliazione 52–54, just outside Piazza San Pietro, was blessed and inaugurated by Cardinal Amleto Giovanni Cicognani, Vatican Secretary of State. The technical equipment provided in the pressroom was excellent, if one overlooks such minor difficulties as not having typewriters with the keyboard differences proper to various languages.

The pressroom had forty typewriters, three duplicating machines, two television sets for viewing ceremonies, thirty telephone booths for local, national, and international service, with a switchboard staffed by multilingual operators provided by the Italian state telephone company. Besides, the pressroom offered eleven Telex machines, cable service, facilities for direct radio transmission of photos, plus telegraph and postal facilities.

Procedures had to be worked out for the accreditation of the immense number of journalists expected for the Council sessions. The first directives issued by the Council Press Office unfortunately aroused widespread resentment. Although the general attitude of the Council Secretariat on which the Press Office then depended was a marked improvement over the mentality of 1869–1870, it did not show the complete openness and spirit of cooperation demanded by effective press relations today.

The directives for accreditation to the Council informed journalists that they could request accreditation provided they could give evidence of the "proper spirit of reverence" in their handling of Council news. Reactions to this statement were immediate and violent. It was interpreted as a forecast that Council journalists would be hobbled by censorship, direct or indirect. Journalists of many countries voiced their dissatisfaction, some even threatening to boycott the proceedings. Perhaps the most dramatic reaction came from the United States, with its long tradition of complete freedom of the press; Monsignor John Kennedy, director of the Information Bureau of the National Catholic Welfare Conference in Washington, resigned rather than translate and transmit such directives to the American press.

Such accreditation requirements indicated that, notwithstanding the elaborate arrangements for press coverage of the Council, there was great danger that the journalists might not have much to report. Certain circles seemed to be under the illusion that in the twentieth century the Church could still discuss and act in secret. Apparently, no one in responsible quarters realized that for the first time in modern history the Vatican was "hot" news. It had never before had to deal with reporters on a large scale. Far too much confidence was placed in the effectiveness of the Council's rule of secrecy to keep all Council discussions under cover.

Revised accreditation procedures were eventually worked out to the satisfaction of all concerned. For Session I of the Council, the Press Office issued 1405 accreditation cards, or *tessere,* to journalists representing almost every country, language, and religion.

Before the opening of the Council, the representatives of the press were given a specially conducted tour of the Council hall in St. Peter's, with detailed explanations by the Vatican engineer who had supervised all the arrangements in the Basilica. They thus had a firsthand view of the setting of the Council discussions as a background for the news that would eventually be forthcoming.

With this background, the Council Press Office was ready to face up to the gigantic task of covering Vatican II.

3

A PRESS OFFICER'S DAY

EACH of the nine language officers of the Council Press Office had full responsibility for publishing the daily news of the Council in his language. He was given complete freedom, limited only by objectivity, both as to what he included in his bulletin and how he expressed it. There was no censorship of any kind. The individual bulletins were not mere carbon copies or translations of the Italian bulletin or of any other. Not infrequently the heads of the different sections checked with one another to insure accuracy, but in the overall performance of his duties each acted on his own responsibility and according to his own methods—methods that were usually dictated by situations within his language group. To our best knowledge, no language officer was ever interfered with in his summation of the Council news. It is important to emphasize the full autonomy guaranteed by the President, Archbishop O'Connor, and all the members of the Episcopal Committee, as well as by Monsignor Vallainc, the Commission's secretary.

The routine day of the Council Press Officers began, along with that of the Council Fathers, with assistance at Holy Mass opening each day's General Congregation at 9 A.M. After the Mass, the regular business session of the Council got under way around 9:45. Each officer was provided with a list of the speakers for the day and also infrequently, when they were available, brief summaries of the discourses to be delivered that morning. The summaries were often practically useless from the news viewpoint, since they lacked both in immediacy and news value.

Since each language-officer was responsible for his own bulletin and could follow any system he wished in taking notes and making reliable summaries, he had to pay close attention to seize the most salient points of the various speeches. Rarely was it possible simply to use the summaries of the texts sometimes furnished by the Secretariat. Frequently a speaker made important last-minute additions in the light of previous discussion. Each speaker had to be followed with the utmost attention, and prolonged periods of such sustained attention—from approximately 9:45 until 12:30 or 12:45—were a great strain. The Press Officers were always happy when the day's agenda called for extended voting, which meant a welcome break in the rugged daily routine of summarizing speeches that followed one another almost without interruption. While one Father spoke, another was "in the wings" and was given the floor as soon as the speaker finished, after the simple announcement of his name and office.

The average number of daily speakers was sixteen, each limited to ten minutes. This was in striking contrast to the General Congregations at Vatican Council I, in which there was no time limit on the speeches of the Council Fathers. Bishop Ullathorne records that the daily average of Fathers speaking was from four to seven! Vatican I held only three General Congregations a week. What this prelate wrote of Vatican I is equally applicable to Vatican II: "We are now fairly launched into work . . . and have had some very able speakers as well as some muffs." But the Press Officers at Vatican II had to pay close attention to them all because of the continuous succession of the speakers.

The Secretariat of the Bishops of England, Wales, Scotland earned the hearty thanks of the English-language bureau and others too. Whenever a Council Father from this group was to address the assembly, its secretary provided full texts of the Latin or the English version for each language section and later had English texts for all journalists present at the oral briefing. Such efficient cooperation facilitated the heavy task of those responsible for dispensing Council news.

When the General Congregation adjourned, the Press Officers were among the first away from the Basilica, hastening to their headquarters at the Council pressroom. Headquarters is perhaps too impressive a word for sections of a mezzanine corridor, set off by screens, and furnished only with a table or two, a couple of chairs, a steel cabinet, a typewriter, and a telephone. Their first task was a quick review of the notes hastily scribbled throughout the morning, to clarify some of the more illegible passages before their imminent meetings with the press.

Within approximately twenty minutes after adjournment each Press Officer met with his journalists for the verbal press communique. This consisted of a quick briefing on each of the morning's speakers and a summary of their more important remarks. The purpose was to enable the wire services and others to get off short reports that could still, for example in the United States, appear in some evening papers that day. The later session of the United States Bishops' Press Panel provided ample opportunity for wide-ranging questions.

Most of the verbal briefings were conducted by the Press Officers. However, some groups arranged to be briefed by one of the Council Fathers just coming from the Basilica. The English-language journalists apparently saw no need to make any change in the system adopted for their convenience.

After the oral briefing, work was begun immediately on the text of the daily printed bulletin. The various Press Officers did not follow the same patterns in preparing their bulletins, because not all had the same deadlines. The English-language bureau was pressed hardest mainly because of evening deadlines in the United States and Canada. The verbal briefing usually began shortly before 1:00 P.M. and ended around 1:30 or 1:35. The bureau aimed at having copies of the printed bulletin as soon as possible after the Press Panel

A Press Officer's Day

opened its discussions at 3:00 P.M. The English-language Press Officer dictated the text of the bulletin from his morning's notes to a typist who cut stencils directly. The English-language typists were Miss Eileen O'Laughlin and Mrs. Marjorie Weeke. These secretaries, along with other essential office help were generously provided by the special Council office of the Bishops of the United States, through the kind cooperation of Monsignor Paul Marcinkus of Chicago, member of the Vatican Secretariat of State. The bulletin covered all the news items of the morning's Congregation and provided ample summaries of all the discourses.

Top priority for the printed bulletin was given to the Press Panel, which always got the first one hundred and fifty copies. Copies were also provided to Vatican Radio for its daily newscast in English at 4:00 P.M. It was rare that the Press Panel meeting broke up at four o'clock without the bulletins having reached those present in time for at least a quick glance. Assistance in such work as sorting the pages and stapling the texts was provided by staff members of the National Catholic Welfare Conference's special Rome office organized to serve the American Bishops during the Council.

The Council news bulletin in English eventually reached a daily circulation of approximately 1750 copies, in contrast to the three or four hundred of the earlier sessions. In addition to the press it served many bishops as a handy review of the daily meetings and a brief resumé of all the discussions and votes. A large number of copies was regularly available for distribution in the Council pressroom beginning at 4:30 P.M., but the demand was so great that distribution had to be restricted to those presenting their *tesserino* as accredited journalists. At their request, bulletins were furnished also to the Canadian bishops, the Indian bishops, the East African bishops, the Secretariat for Christian Unity on behalf of the Observers and Guests, to the Lay Auditors, and to the CCCC (Coordination Center for Council Communications), a super-bureau that endeavored to organize the activities of the different National Documentation Centers.

By the time the last copies of the bulletin were put together, stapled, and distributed, the afternoon was well along. The English-language staff was usually ready to close shop around 4:15 P.M.—ready to begin again the next day.

4

THE U.S. BISHOPS' PRESS PANEL

ALTHOUGH the United States Bishops' Press Panel functioned as an autonomous unit not officially connected with the Council Press Office, no account of press relationships at Vatican II can omit an account of the Panel's work and a warm tribute to its vital contribution to the English-language press throughout the Council. This Press Panel was organized shortly before the opening of the Council in 1962 by the Press Bureau of the National Catholic Welfare Conference, then under the chairmanship of the Most Reverend Albert Zuroweste, Bishop of Belleville, Illinois. It aimed to assemble a corps of ecclesiastical and theological experts to be available on a regularly scheduled basis to the representatives of the English-language press. Being for the most part laymen, the journalists could hardly be expected to have the doctrinal and historical background necessary to understand the broad implications of the Council deliberations. Even clerical journalists would have had some difficulty having always at their fingertips all the wealth of information which the pooled resources of the Press Panel brought to them daily.

The initial Panel was composed of the following members, all of them Council *periti:*

Chairman: The Reverend Edward L. Heston, C.S.C., Procurator and Postulator General of the Congregation of Holy Cross, Consultor of the Sacred Congregation of Religious, author, collaborator in several Curial offices of the Holy See.

Dogmatic Theology: The Reverend John P. McCormick, S.S., Washington, D. C., Rector of the Theological College, The Catholic University of America.

Moral Theology: The Reverend Francis J. Connell, Redemptorist, Washington, D. C., former Dean of the School of Sacred Theology at The Catholic University of America, long recognized as among the foremost theologians of the United States.

Sacred Scripture: The Reverend Francis J. McCool, S.J., New York City, Professor at the Pontifical Biblical Institute in Rome.

The Reverend Eugene H. Maly, Professor at Mount Saint Mary's Seminary, West Norwood, Ohio, President of the Catholic Biblical Association, Editor of the *Bible Today* magazine.

Canon Law: The Reverend William H. Keeler of the Matrimonial Tribunal of the Harrisburg, Pa., Diocese.

Liturgy: The Reverend Frederick H. McManus, Boston, Mass., Consultor of the Conciliar Liturgical Commission, former President of the United States

Liturgical Commission, Professor of Canon Law at The Catholic University of America.

Church History: The Reverend Robert Trisco, Chicago, Professor of Church History at The Catholic University of America, and Associate Editor of *The Catholic Historical Review.*

Ecumenism: The Reverend John B. Sheerin, C.S.P., New York City, Editor of the *Catholic World* and official observer of the Holy See at the World Council of Churches.

The general aim of this panel of experts was well described by a correspondent of *The New York Times* in a feature article that referred to it as "a school of theology for journalists." Wrote Monsignor Walter Tappe in the San Francisco *Monitor:* "Actually, the Bishops have established a quasi-school where some of the finest minds in Rome discuss the subject which the Council Fathers have just debated, and then answer any and all questions from the floor."

At the beginning of the Council the schedule called for the Panel to meet with the press about a half-hour after adjournment of the General Congregation. Meetings were held in the basement assembly hall of the nearby USO Club at the end of Via della Conciliazione. Before long, however, it was clear that this arrangement was not entirely satisfactory. With only the Italian bulletin as a starting point and not having been present for the discussions in the Council Hall, the journalists felt that they were not sufficiently well prepared to propose meaningful questions to the Panel members. Before the end of Session I it was decided to move the panel meetings to 2:30 P.M., allowing ample time for the basic English briefing and also (a point not to be overlooked) for a bite to eat. The Panel meetings were to last just one hour, to enable the correspondents to file their wire stories before their daily deadlines.

The scanty news content of the daily Press Office bulletins during Session I—even the English bulletins had to be translations of the Italian—gave a special significance to the Panel meetings during that period. Not having any news of substance on which to be briefed in depth, the press understandably used the Panel meetings as fishing expeditions, making undisguised efforts to land an occasional substantial news item. Inasmuch as everyone was suffering in varying degrees from the strictures of the Council news policy, it was also evident that Panel members were using their participation in the discussions to impart indirectly news not otherwise available. In spite of the shortcomings and regrettable working conditions not of their making, the gentlemen of the press and the gentlemen of the Panel gradually worked out a very pleasant relationship. One of the contributions of the sessions with the Panel was to show the journalists that someone was anxious to help them tell the Council story to a deeply interested world.

At the beginning of Session II, Father Heston was transferred from the chairmanship of this panel to a new post as English-language Press Officer for the Council. He was succeeded on the Press Panel by Father John B. Sheerin, C.S.P.

The entire atmosphere of the Panel meetings was affected by the new official press policy promulgated in the autumn of 1963. No longer obliged to dig for news, the press was able to use the Panel for its basic original purpose of information in depth. The news stories out of Rome concerning the Council very soon reflected the new situation.

Beginning in Session II a new work schedule was introduced for the Press Panel. Within a quarter-hour after the close of the morning Council meeting, the English-language Press Officer met with the correspondents for a rapid rundown of the day's discussions and newsworthy events, as described in the previous chapter. Because of time limitations, no questions were allowed beyond a quick request for clarification of some detail. As another time-saving measure, copies of page one of the provisory Italian bulletin were distributed; this page listed the names of the speakers and thus obviated the necessity of spelling out unfamiliar names. At the end of this briefing, Father Robert Trisco took over to answer urgent pertinent questions, making it possible for initial stories to be filed without delay.

During Session II the meetings of the Panel were pushed back still further to 3:00 P.M. Every effort was made to have first copies of the English bulletin ready for distribution as soon as possible after the opening of the discussion. As soon as the first 150 copies were ready, Miss Mary Ingoldsby, of the NCWC Bishops' Office, hurried to the USO Club and the waiting and impatient gentlemen of the press. Circumstances beyond the control of the Press Office sometimes upset this schedule, but the press already had the information furnished in the verbal briefing, which could serve as a starting point for Panel discussions.

This procedure was continued in Sessions III and IV. At the beginning of Session III, the chairmanship of the Panel was assumed by Mr. Elmer Von Feldt, News Editor from NCWC headquarters in Washington, D. C., who had participated in an advisory capacity in Session II. Some new members were also added to the Panel:

Education: Monsignor Mark Hurley, Chancellor, Diocese of Stockton, California.

Dogmatic Theology: Father John King, Oblates of Mary Immaculate, of Lowell Mass., Superior of the Oblate House of Studies in Rome.

Dogmatic Theology: Monsignor George W. Shea, Rector, Immaculate Conception, Darlington, N. J.

Theology and Ecumenism: Father George Tavard, Assumptionist Fathers, Chairman, Theology Department, Mt. Mercy College, Pittsburgh, Pa.

An excellent form of journalistic assistance provided by the Bishops' Press Panel was the regular invitations to noted speakers to address the meeting briefly on topics of current Council interest. As often as possible, any English-speaking Father who addressed the Council was invited to the Panel meeting on the same day to enlarge on his remarks and to answer pertinent questions from the floor. Among these, before his untimely death, Father Gustav Weigel, S.J., was a frequent visitor, enlivening the discussions with his dry humor and wry remarks on persons and things, as also such Council Fathers as Bishop John Wright, of Pittsburgh, Bishop Ernest Primeau of Manchester, N. H., Bishop Robert Treacy of Baton Rouge, La. In addition to Council Fathers some of the *periti* addressed the panel: Msgr. George Higgins, Head of the Social Action Bureau of the NCWC, Father Barnabas Ahern, C.P., Scripture scholar, and Father George Tavard, A.A., well-known specialist in ecumenism. Without the Press Panel, these Council figures might have been left in the Olympian isolation encouraged by the general Council atmosphere.

It was interesting to see how most of the journalists very quickly learned the new vocabulary and modes of thought to which the Council was exposing them. It is a long step from the daily beat of local or international news to the apparently detached realm of theology, but more than one correspondent became genuinely interested in such previously unheard-of questions as the source, or sources, of Divine Revelation, in the sometimes bewildering terminology of the Constitution on the Sacred Liturgy, or even in the theological implications for such fields as the media of social communications. On some occasions a particularly well-informed journalist was able to provide an historical or practical detail that had momentarily escaped even the experts on the Panel.

It was the generally accepted conviction of competent observers that the United States Bishops' Press

Panel for the English-language journalists was the perfect answer to the press problems of Vatican II. It provided its own compensations for the time and effort expended in transmitting Council news to the press of the English-speaking world.

5

SESSION I
(October 11—December 7, 1962)

WITH a solemn splendor rarely seen even in the central Basilica of Christendom, Pope John XXIII opened the Second Ecumenical Vatican Council on October 11, 1962, Feast of the Maternity of the Blessed Virgin Mary. Thanks to the press tickets provided by the office of the Majordomo of the Vatican, the journalists, the radio and television correspondents were able to view the inaugural ceremony from special seats. Because the correspondents were in the Basilica that day no special news bulletin was published, although the Press Office provided the journalists with translations of the complete text of the opening Allocution of the Holy Father. The next day, October 12, 1962, the work of the Council Press Office and its seven language-bureau chiefs swung into high gear.

According to the work-plan drawn up previously, a daily oral briefing of the press would be held almost immediately after the Council meeting. At that time there was no authorization for the language-bureau chiefs to be present in St. Peter's during the General Congregations, so the basic source of this initial information was the ample but uninformative bulletin prepared by the Council Secretariat and issued daily soon after adjournment. These bulletins in Italian were actually so jejune, newsless and noncommittal that some journalists remarked, and not at all facetiously, that they gave every indication of having been written before the discussions took place. For example, toward the end of Session I, the momentous and historic speech of Bishop De Smedt, of Bruges, Belgium, flaying the juridicism, clericalism, and triumphalism of the original Constitution on the Church was reported so innocuously that without other sources of information beyond the Press Office bulletin the world would never have realized that there had been a discourse that was to leave a lasting mark on Vatican II.

The Press Officers were expected to translate these bulletins into their respective languages and to make the text available to the journalists. Even in the translating they were working under the evident handicap of reporting on something they had not seen and heard directly. There was nothing in the text to link ideas with the men who proposed them, or any of the other concrete items that make "news" in the commonly accepted sense. For example, no one would ever have suspected that behind some of the drab generalities there lay a vibrant speech by a bishop from the Congo or from Indonesia, pleading for liturgical changes that would take into account their national or tribal cul-

Session I

tures or that a bishop from behind the Iron Curtain had explained, almost tearfully, that liturgical services had to be vitalized since they are his only link with the youth of his diocese.

The following extract from a news bulletin is an example of the "un-news" communiques:

> The first speeches of the assembly touched upon the project on the Sacred Liturgy as a whole in which there were a diversity of opinions expressed. The different tendencies reflect different schools of the liturgical movement, different experiences and problems, which reveal, however, an identical concern for affirming the intrinsic value of the liturgy and to make it the living and real expression of the worship which the universal Church renders to God. . . . The liturgical problem is today the center of an ever greater and noticeable attention. There have come requests for more or less drastic reforms from many areas.

Another bulletin, No. 4, provided the press with a doctrinal explanation of the role of the liturgy:

> The work of Redemption, pre-announced by God in Sacred Scripture and carried out by Christ, is continued in the Church especially through the Liturgy, with the Sacrifice of the Cross renewed perpetually on the Altar, and through the Sacraments, with the daily tribute of public prayer.

Exact and authentic as these statements may be, they hardly represent what the press thinks of as news.

Faced with the impossibility of securing substantial and newsworthy stories, not a few correspondents were recalled by their home offices, and Council coverage suffered appreciably. Those whose task was to provide news of the Council were reduced to devious means of keeping their editors and readers up to date. The inevitable weakening of responsible coverage resulted in a rash of articles and books purporting to give the "inside story" of Vatican II. The situation was in many ways identical to that already described for Vatican I.

Before long it was evident that no measures could keep news of the Council from trickling out—when it did not come flowing out in torrents. It was becoming clear that divisions of opinion could not be ignored, that a sharp drawing of lines on questions could not be quietly glossed over as an "expression of varying opinions." The Council Hall was alive with conflicting currents, at times resulting in clashes; far from being something to be hidden in shame, these facts emphasized the authentic vitality of the Church today. We have only to recall the conciliar tugs-of-war that resulted in the historic Constitution on the Sacred Liturgy and in the Constitution on the Church to have some idea of the forces in conflict, forces and conflicts that it was impossible to hide from the world and absolutely unnecessary to hide under the guise of protecting the image of the Church. Far from being scandalized by information on disagreements and controversies, the press and the world regarded all this as a healthy sign. The days of alleged monolithic unity were numbered. As always happens, a small minority at times exaggerated these elements, but this risk must be regarded as part of the price. Vatican II was gradually finding itself, and a real awakening was being sensed throughout the entire Church. This was news of the highest value. But the press corps was on the outside, thwarted in its efforts to find out honestly what was going on inside.

Despite the unfavorable conditions, the Council Press Office did its best to meet the needs of the press during Session I. Forty-one daily bulletins in Italian were published, totaling 140 mimeographed pages. They were published daily in their entirety in *L'Osservatore Romano*. During this Session eleven press conferences were given by specially selected Council Fathers to treat more fully topics under current discussion. Because of the varying shades of interpretation of the rule of Council secrecy, not all of these press conferences were worthwhile.

Every Sunday a special Mass was celebrated in the chapel of Sant'Ivo, the Renaissance church of the old University of Rome for journalists of all religions. The celebrants of these Masses, for the most part Cardinals, represented various nations or language groups, and their sermons stressed various responsibilities of the press for the diffusion of truth. This Mass was eventually discontinued during Session II because of frequent conflict with ceremonies in St. Peter's on Sunday mornings and also to give the journalists more free time on their much-needed weekly day of rest.

In October, 1962, the special telephone service installed for the Council press representatives handled about 1100 calls, of which 900 were international and 200 national. The telegraph service sent out 550 messages, received over 100, and arranged 35 Telex communications.

In the first month only of the Council, the Italcable service filed approximately 700,000 words for non-European countries and an average of ten radiophotos per day. These services were also available for program broadcasting for a total of approximately 7000 minutes. Telephone conversations on various lines totaled 700,000 minutes. During the second month of the Council, the pace of these services decreased noticeably, although it still maintained high figures.

From October 8 until October 31, 1962, the Press Radio service transmitted 294,982 words, of which 214,000 went by Telex to Europe, 48,000 on the internal Italian network, and 32,000 to the United States. This pace continued almost unvaried throughout the Council session.

The mobile post office, set up by the Italian government in the vicinity of the Press Office in Piazza Pio XII, sent to outgoing trains or planes more than 10,000 letters in the first month of the Council, along with 90,000 post cards, 32,000 letters and cards via air mail, plus 400 telegrams, 600 registered letters, and 2000 special delivery letters.

Toward the end of Session I Cardinal Montini spoke in the Council Hall on the schema dealing with the Church. His words are generally cerdited with having played a vital role in determining the general tone of this important document and in making it the keystone of Vatican II. The chairman of the Press Panel wrote to the Cardinal, who had been obliged to return to Milan some days before adjournment, asking him if he would make his text available to the press.

His Eminence had been greatly displeased with the treatment given one of his weekly news letters from the Council to his diocesan newspaper. The letter had been widely misunderstood, not to say distorted by certain sectors of the press, to the point of attributing to the Cardinal appreciations of the Council and of the Roman Curia that he had never formulated. His disappointment at this unexpected treatment was reflected in his reply here translated from the Italian. After an opening sentence with personal recollections, the Cardinal's letter said:

Milano, December 14, 1962

Very Reverend Father,

... As for my part in the Council discussions, I cannot provide any information, nor do I think it would be really worthwhile.

There have been certain reports based on an unfriendly and, to my way of thinking, unobjective press regarding a family letter on the Council written by me from Rome to the people of my diocese. I am sending you the text for your own information, but I would not want to see any further discussion of the matter. ...

✠ G. B. Card. Montini
Archbishop

Session I was brought to a close by Pope John XXIII on December 7, 1962, in an atmosphere made sombre by persistent reports of the grave illness of the Pope. The situation of the press had not improved appreciably since the opening of the Session on October 11. The general feeling was that, unless there were radical changes in the following Session, the Council could not fail to lose prestige before world opinion. The Council whose goal was to bring the Church into step with modern times could hardly expect to achieve this while practically ignoring such a medium as the world press. Session I had come to a close; Session II was a question mark as far as the press was concerned.

6

SESSION II

(September 29—December 4, 1963)

BETWEEN the end of Session I and the opening of Session II the Church and the entire world were saddened by the death of "good Pope John." Session II, originally scheduled to begin September 14, 1963, opened on September 29, after a brief postponement reflecting almost to the day the period between the death of Pope John XXIII and the election of Pope Paul VI. The launching of this Session marked a genuine change in relationships between the Council and the press. The new state of affairs had not just happened over night.

Journalists had not been alone in recognizing the deficiencies of press policy during the first Session. Steps aimed at a drastic revision of prevailing procedures were taken shortly after its close. After prolonged discussion and careful study, the Press Office submitted a report to the Co-ordinating Commission of the Council on March 29, 1963. It dealt with three subjects: 1) the work done by the Press Office during the Preparatory Period and during the initial Session of the Council; 2) the question of Council secrecy; 3) possible solutions of the press problem for future Sessions.

This report was followed on July 4, 1963, with a memorandum outlining a plan for improving the information services of the Council. The plan called for the organization, if not of a new Council organism, at least of a special Commission to determine the scope and character of the news to be made available to the press. This plan was the result of consultations with various Council Fathers in the light of the largely unhappy experience of Session I. The Co-ordinating Commission approved the general outline of the plan and asked that it be implemented in time for the coming Session II.

The plan at first called for the appointment of a Cardinal to supervise the work of the Press Office and assume ultimate responsibility for Council press relations. The Cardinal would have been able to make effective use of his contacts among the Council Fathers. He would act as Secretary for the meetings of the new press body and be responsible for the actualization of any plans decided upon. The final decision was for a prelate other than a Cardinal, who would have the confidence of both the Council Fathers and the press.

As president of this special Episcopal Commission, Pope Paul VI chose Archbishop Martin J. O'Connor, of Scranton, Pa., then Rector of the Pontifical North American College in Rome and President of the Pontifical Secretariat for the Media of Social Communication. Archbishop O'Connor was in the United States

Session II 57

when notified of this important assignment. Before long, he was back in Rome at work.

From the outset, the President of the new Episcopal Commission for the Press was assured of the wholehearted cooperation and encouragement of the Holy Father. In a long private audience, the Archbishop set before His Holiness the main outlines of a radically new Council press policy.

According to the new policy, the heads of the language bureaus were to assist at all Council meetings in St. Peter's Basilica. They were to have access to the various schemas and all other Council documents and, when such texts were available, to the discourses of the Fathers addressing the Council. The obligation of secrecy was restricted to the actual texts of the documents under discussion and to the discussions in the various Commissions. The highlight of the new policy was authorization for the Council Press Officers *to report to their respective language groups everything said and done in the Council hall.* A new and immeasurably brighter era had dawned for the world press covering Vatican II.

The first members appointed to the Episcopal Commission for the Press in early September, 1963, reflected a wide geographical and linguistic representation:

Archbishop René Stourm, of Sens (France)
Archbishop Andrea Pangrazio of Gorizia (Italy)
Archbishop Engene D'Souza, of Bhopal (India)
Archbishop Owen McCann, of Capetown (South Africa), later Cardinal

Archbishop Hyacinthe Thiandoum, of Dakar, Senegal, for the various African episcopates.

Bishop Joseph Khoury of Tyr (Lebanon)

Bishop Albert Zuroweste, of Belleville, Illinois (USA)

Bishop Helmut Wittler of Osnabruck (Germany)

Bishop José Girarda, Auxiliary Bishop of Seville (Spain)

Bishop Mark McGrath, C.S.C., Auxiliary of Panama City, for Spanish Latin America

Bishop Joao Rezendo Costa (Brazil), for Portuguese

Bishop Gerhard De Vet of Breda (Holland)

Bishop Luigi Baccino of San José de Mayo (Uruguay) later succeeded Bishop McGrath, who resigned because of pressing duties on the Theological Commission

Bishop Henri Routhier, O.M.I., Vicar Apostolic of Grouard (Alberta) for the Canadian press.

In his press conference on the eve of the opening of Session II, Archbishop O'Connor summed up the aims of the Episcopal Commission: Either through the individual members or through the Council Press Office to facilitate the publication of the daily news bulletins; to help organize the official weekly press conferences; to provide doctrinal assistance for the various National Documentation Centers, and to direct further daily contacts with newspapers and other news media accredited to the Council Press Office. In a word the Episcopal Commission for the Press was to serve as the official link between the Council organisms and public opinion through the facilities of the Council Press Office. The press would henceforth not depend on the

Council Secretariat. The headquarters of the Press Commission were established in the Palazzo San Carlo, in Vatican City, in connection with the main offices of the Pontifical Secretariat for Press, Radio, Television and the Cinema.

After Session I, because of pressure of his duties as Head of the NCWC News Bureau in Rome, Monsignor James Tucek resigned as English-language Press Officer for the Council. He was succeeded by the Rev. Edward L. Heston, C.S.C., Procurator General of the Congregation of Holy Cross, long resident in Rome and well acquainted with the background of Vatican activities and the Roman Curia. Father Heston took over his new duties at the opening of Session II, just as the new and enlightened Council press policy was to take effect.

A special press table was set up in St. Peter's, behind that assigned to the Council Secretariat and not far from the long table occupied by the twelve Cardinals of the Council Presidency. Each of the Press Officers was responsible for taking his own notes, although all collaborated to make it possible for the provisory Italian bulletin to be immediately available to the Press Officers at the end of the daily meetings. In this collaboration Press Officers were assigned a certain number of speakers to be "covered" during the morning and to be summarized in brief notes in Italian. These notes were gone over by the Italian Press Officer to assure correctness and evenness of style and were then turned over to a special assistant to the Italian-language officer who was set up in a distant corner of the Basilica typing stencils as the summaries were turned over to him. When the General Congregation adjourned there were only one or two discourses to be summarized and stenciled before sending the bulletin on for quick mimeographing. Thus the Italian basic bulletin, for those who wished to use it, was ready for the different language bureaus within minutes after the Council Fathers left the Basilica. Some of the Press Officers, however, preferred to turn out their own bulletins, to eliminate the danger of stilted style and other drawbacks so difficult to avoid in hasty translations.

Because of the official nature of the daily printed news bulletins, there was a ban on direct attribution to individuals. In the preliminary verbal briefing, however, this restriction was not applicable since it was not official. A system was eventually worked out to avoid attributing remarks incorrectly. The day's speakers were listed in the bulletin in chronological order of appearance and numbered. The summaries of the discourses and interventions were given a corresponding number as each speaker was recorded. Although not foolproof (and certainly unofficial), it added greatly to the news value of Press Office reports and made it possible for newsmen to call special attention to local Council Fathers in various parts of the world. These declarations on the Council floor often took on special significance when it was known, even unofficially, which Council Fathers were responsible for them.

Nothing will provide a clearer idea of the difference in Council press releases than a comparison of the first and second bulletins of Session II. Bulletin 1 of that Session was prepared according to the procedure followed in Session I, basing the release on the Italian bulletin, with no attempt at unofficial identification of the speakers. Bulletin 2, on the contrary, was written with full use of the new press policy. Texts of these two strikingly different bulletins are found in the Appendix to this present volume.

It would be difficult to describe adequately the general lightening of the atmosphere when the new press policy was effectively implemented. Gone was the discouragement that had been so palpable in 1962. There was a new enthusiasm among the journalists who could secure their news without recourse to roundabout and unreliable devices. They felt they were getting an even break. Communications media throughout the world soon reflected the "new look" in Council press service. One journalist remarked that in Session I, after the excitement of the opening days, any of his stories that were used at all had been relegated to the inside pages, whereas in Session II he was making page one every day.

The new press policy made no provision for the presence of newsmen inside the Basilica for the Council sessions, and this at first caused some complaints. These, however, appeared to be mostly pro forma. Very few of the journalists accredited to the Council had the minimum practical grasp of Latin essential to follow the speeches intelligently for later summary and comment. Most newsmen saw a practical advantage in their exclusion. As one remarked, there was no particular reason why they should sit through the morning-long sessions to get material when an official Council spokesman gave it to them ready-made a short time after adjournment.

During Session II, 41 daily news bulletins appeared, each of them more lengthy and detailed than any appearing in Session I. Five press conferences on Council issues were held by different Council Fathers.

The end of Session II saw a practical example of the new kind of cooperation between the Press Office and the journalists. It was expected that the Public Session would be marked by the promulgation of the Constitution on the Sacred Liturgy and by an important Allocution of the Pope, which confronted several of the journalists with a concrete problem. The closing ceremonies were scheduled for Wednesday morning, December 4, 1963, and the papers would have to handle on one day the closing ceremonies, the Constitution on the Liturgy, and the Allocution of the Holy Father. A request was made that translations of the liturgical Constitution be made available in advance with a strict embargo on release so that explanatory notes could be prepared beforehand. Thus the journalists and their home editors could concentrate on the closing of the Session and the discourse of Pope Paul VI. The Press Office cooperated wholeheartedly and made the text of the Constitution available. Any such collaboration would have been unthinkable in Session I.

Shortly after the opening of Session II, several journalists representing agencies and individual papers, as well as some other interested groups, sent a letter of appreciation to Pope Paul VI through Archbishop Martin O'Connor. They thanked the Pope for the progressive measures adopted in their behalf and the professional consideration afforded them. The report of the Press Office to the Co-ordinating Commission lists the following signers: The German Documentation Center; The France Presse agency; *The Christian Century; The Catholic Weekly; The Western Michigan Catholic; The New York Times; Die Presse* of Vienna; The National Association of the Spanish Press Association; The Director of the Spanish Press; *Time* magazine; *The New York Herald Tribune; The New Republic;* Vatican Radio; *Commonweal; Jubilee; America;* UPI; *The Minneapolis Star; The Long Island Catholic; The Universe;* The Australian Catholic Press Association; *Newsweek; The Catholic Herald;* The Information Director of the Ecumenical Council of Churches; The Press Syndicate of Lebanon; the embassies of the United Arab Republic, Iraq, Syria, and Yemen.

It was during Session II that a Council document directly affecting the press came up for discussion. This was the schema of the decree on the Social Media of Communication. Toward the end of Session I the document had been sent back to the appropriate commission for thorough revision; the Council Fathers had found it inadequate, despite its length, and wanted it compressed into a more succinct form better adapted to the needs of communications media in these modern times. Although the schema as submitted to Session II was a notable improvement in many ways, many competent professionals still found it wanting in one or several respects. A petition signed by a large number of accredited journalists was circulated unofficially among the Council Fathers, calling several specific points to their attention and suggesting respectfully that the schema not be approved. Although this move was not successful, it did provide the press with an opportunity to express its mind as forcefully as possible on a subject in which they rightfully regarded themselves as having special competence and interest.

One of the most dramatic moments of Session II for the press was the announcement that Pope Paul VI was to travel as a pilgrim to the Holy Land in prayer for the Council, for the Church, and for the entire world. On the closing day of the Session the various Press Officers had assembled to receive copies of the Pope's Allocution bringing the Session to an end. At first sight, the text seemed somewhat on the short side, and, in addition, the conclusion was quite different from any other—none of the usual formulas imparting the Apostolic Benediction or anything of the kind. The natural impulse was simply to attribute this to a new look in papal discourses.

Later in the morning the Press Officers were convoked in great secrecy in a secluded corner of the Press headquarters. There the Secretary distributed the remainder of the Allocution containing the announcement of the historic pilgrimage, the first ever made from Rome to the Holy Land by any Pope. The text was to be translated immediately, mimeographed, and held in absolute secrecy until the Holy Father read the actual paragraph. With the approach of the moment for the dramatic disclosure, it was evident that rumors had leaked out. As the Press Officers made their way to the press room, one journalist leaned out of a phone booth to say excitedly that London was on the line asking for a confirmation of the report that had just come over the wires. Another inquired with nonchalant incredulity if there was anything to "the utterly fantastic rumor" that the Pope was going to the Holy Land.

The actual announcement stunned the assembled journalists. Commotion in the pressroom was indescribable as the correspondents raced for the phone booths to get the announcement to their home offices. From that moment on there was no other subject of conversation. Before the morning was over, two prominent journalists were already seated at a table with the English-language Press Officer, asking questions and mapping plans to cover the epoch-making visit in order to write "the best possible story," as they put it, on the Pope and his visit to the homeland of Christ.

Pope Paul VI had really shown the press a thing or two. Many have remarked that not even publicity specialists from Madison Avenue could have used the press more adroitly or with more telling effect than did Pope Paul in announcing his forthcoming unprecedented pilgrimage. It was becoming a commonplace among the journalists that it was impossible for any secret to be well kept among the Council personnel of nearly three thousand bishops and *periti*. But the Pope had demonstrated that one man, planning things well and practically, can keep a secret even from the press until the right psychological moment has come. The simple fact that Pope Paul had decided to make this public announcement of his plans was itself an eloquent testimony to the change of news policy of which Session II had been the happy witness.

At this Session the Press Office, through the President of the Council Commission for the Press, had issued accreditation cards to 518 new journalists, over and above those previously approved. Interesting also is the log of the special services provided by the Council Press Room. This office handled 3414 outgoing telephone calls and 590 incoming calls, for ten European countries and two countries outside Europe. The Press radio service transmitted 794,650 words for ten countries in Europe and the two Americas. The telegraph division sent out 2204 telegrams, containing 29,745 words, to twelve European countries, as well as 2200 telegrams with 361,470 words, to destinations in nineteen non-European countries, and received 336 incoming wires. The intercontinental telephone service handled approximately 416 hours of conversation.

In most instances these special services did double the work performed in Session I, indicating to what extent the revised news policy had actually assured a much wider diffusion of Council information. Whereas the Press wireless service had transmitted approximately 295,000 words in the month of October, 1962, in Session I, its total output for Session II came to something like 795,000 words, a remarkable increase. However, there were no complaints that the capacity of the news services was being overtaxed.

Religious News Service Photo

Pope John XXIII addresses some 1000 newsmen covering Vatican Council II. Seated before Michelangelo's fresco of *The Last Judgment* in the Sistine Chapel, the Pope told journalists that the Council is "essentially a great religious event," and he asked their cooperation in reporting it truthfully and without sensationalism. "The distortion of the truth by the organs of information can have incalculable consequences," he warned.

In the October 13, 1962, address, Pope John also stated that the Roman Catholic Church "has nothing to hide" and has "no political machinations afoot." The Pope is flanked by Federico Callori Di Vignale, Papal Chamberlain, left, and Monsignor Salvatore Capoferri, Master of Pontifical Ceremonies.

Wide World Photo

'May We Quote Your 'No Comment,' Your Excellency?'

Schweitzer

This cartoon was widely circulated in the U.S. Catholic press during the fall of 1962, as a satire on the press policy then prevailing in Session I of the Council.

Religious News Service Photo

Standing before St. Peter's Basilica are the American bishops who were members of the committee that organized the United States Bishops' Press Panel, left to right: Bishop Thomas H. Gorman of Dallas; Auxiliary Bishop Philip M. Hannan of Washington, D.C.; Bishop Albert R. Zuroweste of Belleville, Illinois, committee chairman; Auxiliary Bishop James H. Griffith of New York; and Bishop John J. Wright of Pittsburgh.

S. Appetiti
English-language journalists being briefed after a General Congregation during Session II by their Press Officer, Rev. Edward L. Heston, C.S.C.

Religious News Service Photo

Father Heston is pictured at another briefing session for English-language journalists during Session II. The daily oral briefings lasted for approximately 30 minutes; the newsmen were also furnished with an official bulletin in English.

Pope Paul VI addresses the assembled press corps at the Sala Stampa on November 26, 1965, prior to the closing of the final session of Vatican II.

With the initation of the new press policy at the beginning of Session II, the staff of the Council Press Office included, left to right, seated: Rev. Francesco Farusi, S.J. (Italian), Rt. Rev. Msgr. Gerhard Fittkau (German), Rt. Rev. Msgr. Fausto Vallainc (Secretary of the Episcopal Commission for the Press and Director of the Office), Rev. François Bernard, A.A. (French), Rev. Edward L. Heston, C.S.C. (English); standing: Rev. Cipriano Calderon (Spanish), Rev. Paolo Almeida, S.J. (Portuguese), Rev. Ambrose Am-Po Ly (Chinese), Rev. Stefan Wesoly (Polish), and Rev. Munged Achem (Arabic).

S. Appetiti

A view of part of the Basilica showing the position of the Press Officers: foreground, section for the Cardinals; small table in center, Moderators; small table on the right, General Secretary and Under-secretaries; long table, Council Presidency; on the right behind the long table, Council Secretariat, Press Officers, various aides.

Religious News Service Photo
During the Council's Session III, American journalists receive a briefing by members of the U.S. Bishops' Press Panel, whose members were available for lectures on the workings of the Council.

Felici

In the Palace of St. Charles in Vatican City, the Episcopal Commission for the Press meets with the Press Officers for the various language bureaus—October 17, 1963.

Religious News Service Photo
Members of the U.S. Bishops' Press Panel during Session III were, left to right, top row: Rev. George Tavard, Rev. Francis J. Connell, C.Ss.R., Rev. Francis J. McCool, S.J., and Archbishop Joseph T. McGucken, chairman of the Panel; bottom row: Msgr. George W. Shea, Rev. John J. King, O.M.I., Msgr. Mark J. Hurley, and Rev. Frederick McManus.

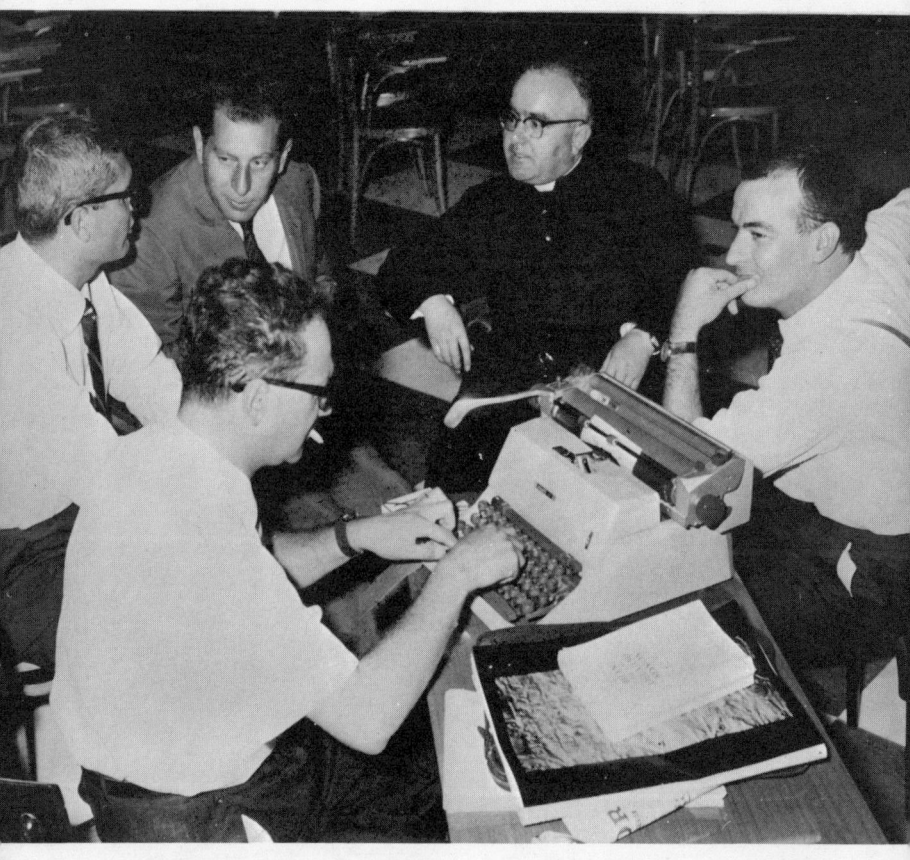

Religious News Service Photo
A scene in press quarters at the opening of Session III. Msgr. Fausto Vallainc, Secretary of the Episcopal Commission for the Press and Director of the Press Office, chats with newsmen during a quiet moment.

Bernard Cardinal Alfrink, Archbishop of Utrecht, addressing journalists at a press conference, October 29, 1965, on the subject, "War and Peace."

7

SESSION III
(September 14—November 21, 1964)

In the ten weeks of Session III of Vatican II, the work pace in the Council Press Office continued as before, and even accelerated. Unlike the preceding two Sessions, Session III had no doldrums. In fact, there were days during the Session when everyone would have warmly welcomed a break. This Session was not interrupted as frequently as Session II had been for such special events as the commemoration of the anniversary of the election of Pope John XXIII on October 28, 1963, the commemoration of the fourth centenary of the Council of Trent, and others. In fact, the Session was marked by such determination not to lose time that, more than once, the regular free day on Saturday was cancelled by the General Secretariat when a holiday had occurred earlier in the week. The historians of the Council will inform further generations on the number of schemas discussed and voted on, the number of Council votes, the number of days devoted to each document, the number of speakers, and other interesting details.

Although this book is not intended to be a chronology of the Council some of the statistics of the Secretariat have at least an indirect bearing on the work of the Press Office. For example, the fact that 659 Fathers took the floor to address the Council, not counting various other discourses by Council officials and Lay Auditors, gives some idea of the volume of work for the Press Office. Each language bureau had to provide summaries of all speeches, which averaged a little more than thirteen for each General Congregation. The record number was reached on September 22, 1964, when nineteen Fathers addressed the assembly.

It was the responsibility of the press to report the results of the 148 votes taken by the Council assembly during this Session. For each of these ballots, some on procedure and some on content, all of which were fortunately tabulated by electronic computers, the press bureaus undertook to provide a capsule statement of the point at issue and the final results of the voting.

During this Session, the Episcopal Commission was following the work of the Press Bureau very actively. It held six plenary meetings on September 29, October 7, 21, and 27, and November 4 and 18. The Commission discussed the format of the weekly official press conferences as well as the choice of speakers. Although unsuccessful in their efforts, the Commission submitted two formal written requests to the General Secretariat asking that groups of journalists be authorized to be present in the Council hall by turn for a General Congregation. There seemed to be some lurking distrust of the press motivating the rejection of these requests.

The greater abundance of available news in Session III was clearly reflected in the daily news bulletins.

The length of this Session produced 48 bulletins, one for each of the General Congregations. The English-language bulletins, instead of the three pages and sometimes less of Session I, usually ran to six and on two occasions even to seven closely packed pages. The total number of pages in the Session's bulletins was close to 270.

An impressive amount of background material was made available through the respective press bureaus. Chief among these documents were the very substantial summaries of the conciliar schemas distributed to the press as the documents came up for discussion. The timing was necessary because of the prohibition against making public the actual texts of the Council schemas, whether in the original Latin or in translation. The texts distributed in the various languages, for the most part prepared by the respective language bureau chiefs, were sufficiently complete to provide an adequate understanding of the theme under discussion, at the same time so expressed not to run afoul of the regulation forbidding translations at the schema stage.

Under the official auspices of the Council Press Office, the following press conferences were held on Saturday mornings during Session III:

September 9, 1964—Archbishop Martin J. O'Connor, President of the Episcopal Commission for the Press: the agenda of the Press Office for Session III.

September 19, 1964—Bishop Carlo Colombo, Tit. Bishop of Vittoriana, President of the Istituto Giuseppe Toniolo, Milan: the schema on The Church.

September 29, 1964—Archbishop John Carmel Heenan, of Westminster, England: the Declaration on Religious Liberty and the Declaration on Non-Christian Religions.

October 3, 1964—Bishop André Charue, of Namur, Belgium: the schema on Divine Revelation.

October 10, 1964—Bishop Manuel Larrain, of Talca, Chile (President of C.E.L.A.M., the International Council of the Episcopal Conferences of Latin America): The Apostolate of the Laity.

October 17, 1964—Bishop Emilio Guano, of Livorno, Italy: on the genesis and the aims of the schema on The Presence of the Church in the Modern World.

October 24, 1964—Bishop John Wright, of Pittsburgh, Pa.: on the first three chapters of the same schema.

November 3, 1964—Monsignors Michele Maccarone and Pietro Silvi, with Dr. Germano Gualdo: to present their volume *The Pilgrimage of Paul VI in the Holy Land*.

Lest the Session be all work and no play, the Council Press Office, on October 31, 1964, offered the journalists a day's outing to Assisi. There the group of about one hundred, representing twenty-four nations, with journalists even from Russia and Czechoslovakia, were luncheon guests of Don Giovanni Rossi at *La Cittadella Cristiana* and were provided with guide service for visits to St. Francis' Basilica and the other major shrines. Traveling via the Autostrada del Sole, the group was back in Rome about 8:30 P.M.

Session III

The growing news possibilities of the Council in Session III resulted in the wider use of the up-to-date means of communication provided by the Press Office. The telephone service handled 3667 outgoing calls for Europe and abroad, along with 761 long-distance calls within Italy. From Europe and abroad 851 incoming calls were received.

The Press radio service dispatched to the Americas 1250 press telegrams amounting to about 850,000 words, and to Europe the Tele-service sent out 1650 messages for a total of two and a half million words, making an over-all total of about 3,350,000 words. The telegraph services transmitted 435 outgoing wires and received 118.

As for the photo services, it is conservatively estimated that about 10,000 pictures were placed on display for eventual orders. These photos taken in the piazza and inside the Basilica before and after the several Congregations—none were allowed during the General Congregations except briefly and on rare occasions—were available to the Council Fathers and to the press. They were exhibited, some in color and some in black and white, on the premises of the Press Office, with attendants available for taking orders.

This brief account of Session III might give the erroneous impression that it reflects a lack of achievement. In fact, however, the work load of Session III was the heaviest of the entire Council, even though the Session was lacking in some of the spectacular developments that had lent such color to Session II. The forty-eight General Congregations set a record unequalled in any of the other Sessions, and this entailed a similar record for the consequent forty-eight bulletins issued by the Press Office. These press releases were supplemented by thirty items of Council documentation, such as summaries of constitutions and decrees and other helpful releases.

It was a tribute to the place won by Vatican II in the framework of lasting news of the twentieth century that on November 30, 1964, the English-language Press Office was asked by the Library of Congress for available new bulletins on the Council.

8

SESSION IV
(September 14—December 8, 1965)

THE fourth and last Session of the Council opened on September 14, 1965, Feast of the Exaltation of the Holy Cross, the anniversary of the opening of Session III. At the beginning of this fourth round the press were very confident that the excellent working relationship established with the Council Press Office since 1963 would continue. This confidence was not deceived.

In Session IV the Council press corps was served by the same language officers as in Session III. No new language bureaus were added.

Even though the Council was moving into its fourth Session—or fourth "period" as the official terminology would have it—new journalists were requesting accreditation, especially for the coverage of such burning issues as religious liberty and the attitude of the Catholic Church toward non-Christian religions, especially the Jews. The attendance of the journalists at the daily briefings continued to be exemplary—from a standing-room-only basis during the discussions on religious liberty to not a few empty chairs during the reports of the National Episcopal Conferences on the proposed revision of the Church's discipline on Indulgences.

The activities of the Council Press Office had begun on Monday, September 13, the eve of the opening of the Session, with a press conference in Italian by Cardinal Julius Doepfner, Archbishop of Munich on "The Outlook for Session IV." Another special conference was held on September 25 by Cardinal Paolo Marella, President of the Council Commission on the Pastoral Duties of Bishops, who spoke in Italian on the Synod of Bishops, of which Pope Paul VI had decreed the erection in his motu proprio *Apostolica Solicitudo,* issued on September 15, 1965.

Acting on the experience acquired during the previous three Sessions, the Press Office decided not to organize the weekly Saturday press conferences of previous years. It was felt that the journalists, not to speak of the Press Officers themselves, would appreciate a week-end break in a consistently trying work schedule. Nevertheless, during the first week-long recess of the Session, October 17–24, a special series of press conferences was organized to discuss the themes that had been under discussion on the Council floor. These conferences were as follows:

October 19, in French, Cardinal Paul Zoungrana, Bishop of Ouagadougou (Upper Volta): "The Chief Problems of the Missions Today."

October 20, in Spanish, the Very Reverend Pedro Arrupe, S.J., Superior General of the Society of Jesus: "Culture and the Missions."

October 22, in Italian, Cardinal Bernard Alfrink, Archbishop of Utrecht and President of the International Association *Pax Christi:* "War and Peace."

During a later recess at the end of November, two further conferences were held:

In French, Archbishop Gabriel Garrone, Archbishop of Toulouse: "The Aims and Limitations of Schema XIII."

In Italian, Archbishop Michele Pellegrino, Archbishop of Torino, Italy: "The Man of Culture and Schema XIII."

Each press conference was usually given in the language of the speaker, although Cardinal Alfrink, of Utrecht, Holland, spoke in Italian in order to reach a wider audience. Most of the speakers were accomplished linguists and could field questions from the floor in several languages. Most of the journalists could thus ask their questions each in his own language, although the Press Officers were always present to help with translations. The usual chairman of the weekly press conferences was Archbishop Martin J. O'Connor, President of the Council Commission for the Press.

The daily press bulletins appeared regularly in their traditional form. The English-language bulletin reached its highest demand with a record daily issue of 1756 copies at the peak of interest during the Session. The length of the bulletins remained much the same, running regularly from five to seven pages. The highest number of Council Orators summarized in any one bulletin was eighteen, one short of the all-Council record of nineteen in Session III. Toward the end of the

Session, after the close of discussion on the Council schemas, the bulletins were noticeably shorter. With only votes to record and bits of daily Council news, and an occasional *Relatio* as a schema was brought in for voting, the bulletins dropped to three and even to two pages.

The press policy adopted in 1963 was responsible for advance authorized translations of documents coming up for solemn voting and promulgation in the four Public Sessions. This enabled the journalists to write more complete stories and to provide more carefully selected quotations from the documents. Had this service not been made available, as the director of one of the major wire services wrote, the bulk of work accumulating on the days of the Public Sessions would have been such that "we would be victims, and so would you." The convenience provided to the press was thus to the advantage of the Council itself.

The experience of the journalists with the Council Press Office was so generally satisfactory that the press representatives who would be remaining in Rome on assignment after the Council wondered what they could expect, once the special arrangements made for the Council had become history. Many veteran Rome hands were very frank in voicing their dread of returning to the old system in which most of the time they were thoroughly frustrated in their efforts to get legitimate Vatican news.

In their desire to provoke concrete action a group of journalists regularly assigned to Rome collaborated in drawing up a formal petition to Pope Paul VI, asking explicitly for the establishment of a regular Vatican Press Office and the appointment of competent personnel to service the Vatican in its relations with the world press too—as is the case with government offices everywhere, with large business organizations, and so forth. The journalists made it clear that their request was motivated only by their desire to provide more effective professional service, which in turn would contribute immeasurably to bettering the "image" of the Vatican before the world. Only time will tell what the results of this initiative may be, but it demonstrated the genuine interest of the responsible press in this center of world news, which the Vatican has become and will certainly remain in the post-conciliar period, as is clear from the far-reaching measures sketched by Pope Paul VI in the allocution with which he closed the eighth Public Session of the Council on November 18.

On Friday, November 26, at 4:30 P.M. the Council press corps was honored by a visit from Pope Paul VI in the pressroom of the Council Press Office headquarters. This unexpected visit by the Pope was the result of steps taken early in the Council to arrange an audience for the journalists and the personnel of the Press Office. In previous Sessions and by force of circumstances the audiences granted to the press had not been at times convenient for all, especially the Press Office staff workers, to attend. Such considerations evidently moved the Holy Father to the unusual step of arranging a final audience in the Council press headquarters and at an hour convenient for everyone.

His Holiness reached the "Sala Stampa" shortly before 4:30 P.M. and was welcomed at the entrance by Archbishop Martin J. O'Connor, President of the Episcopal Commission for the Press, Archbishop Pericle Felici, General Secretary of the Council, and Monsignor Fausto Vallainc, Secretary of the Commission. The Pope was greeted with hearty applause by the approximately five hundred journalists assembled for the occasion. After showing by his gestures his pleasure at being there and his appreciation of the warm welcome, the Pope ascended the throne set up in the pressroom and immediately began to read his prepared address.

Speaking in French, Pope Paul first pointed out that the facilities made available to the press covering the Council had been intended as a proof of the Church's keen interest in their work. He spoke of the enormous volume of work produced by the Council journalists in their response to the demands of "the laws of information." Then an eloquent tribute to the substantial role played by the press in the evolution of the Council: "If the Church has felt, as never before in its two thousand-year history, so many millions of men interested in the meetings of bishops of the entire world, it is without any doubt, dear sirs, to you that this is owed very largely."

The Pope referred briefly to the special problems entailed in affording adequate news coverage for an organization as complex as the Roman Catholic Church, with a nature and a scope belonging entirely to the spiritual order. He gently chided the gentlemen of the press for certain "external presentations," "unfounded hypotheses," and "marginal interpretations" that had characterized some aspects of their Council coverage. But he charitably attributed this to the peculiar difficulties already referred to, while still remarking on the impropriety of dramatizing Church activities through the use of secular terminology and the concepts and categories accepted in everyday life.

Paul VI then gave the assembled journalists the message they were so anxious to hear: "The Holy See is disposed to continue, within the limits of its possibilities, this same service [as for the Council] in such a way that information will be transmitted to you with all the speed and detail demanded by present-day needs and the importance of news."

However, the press was reminded that at times the Vatican must maintain a certain reserve in issuing news, and this for many reasons. The Pope insisted that such necessary reserve implies no attempt to "escape what has become an obligation in the modern world."

Pope Paul was generous in his praise of the staff of the Council Press Office, declaring his desire to pay public tribute to their spirit of zealous dedication and to "their daily work, often unknown and trying, in the service of the press and the service of the truth." The journalists expressed their complete accord in a burst of prolonged applause.

In concluding his address the Holy Father struck a particularly gracious note when he voiced the hope that the future would bring him other opportunities to meet the press. His words were again interrupted by applause. He restated his intention to pursue vigorously the lines of action pointed out by the Council, adding with a sly touch of humor that "this activity of Ours will also serve to increase your work."

On finishing his discourse the Pope came down to greet individually the members of the Episcopal Commission for the Press. He was also to cross to the other side of the throne to greet the various language chiefs, but before he got there the crowd had surged up front and was hemming him in on all sides. It was hardly possible for the language officers to be presented, and not even a brief conversation was possible—self-preservation was more imperative. Someone remarked that the situation was reminiscent of the historic crush at the Damascus gate when the Pope was in the Holy Land! His Holiness finally made his way through the crowd, reaching out his arms in affectionate greeting and almost seeming to want to double their length to reach more eager souls. He left the press building to the cheers of a large crowd gathered outside. Through the visit of Pope Paul VI to their headquarters the Council press corps had received a stamp of approval that would have been scarcely imaginable three years earlier.

A measure of the world's unflagging interest in the work of the Second Vatican Council can be found once more in the statistics reflecting the activities of the technical services set up for the Council. Session IV was responsible for 892 long-distance telephone calls within Italy and for 3141 international and intercontinental calls. Fifty-eight telegrams were received at the Press Office, and 706 were dispatched. The total number of words transmitted by the Press wireless service was 5,250,000, bringing to the impressive total of close to ten million the words sent out by this service reporting on the Council's activities since October 11, 1962.

Toward the end of Session IV the Council Press Office sponsored a special exposition of Council photography from all sources, covering the period from the very beginning of Session I. Close to two hundred photos were submitted in competition, to be judged by a special jury headed by Bishop Giovanni Fallani, President of the Pontifical Commission for Sacred Art. The exposition was artistically arranged in the picturesque ancient church of Saint Lawrence *in piscibus,* popularly known as "San Lorenzino" or "little Saint Lawrence." The high quality of the many photos drew an impressive number of visitors, culminating in the visit of Pope Paul VI on November 26, 1965, immediately after his address to the journalists in the nearby "Sala Stampa." Five cash prizes were awarded to photographers from the United States (first prize), Italy and France (a husband-and-wife team winning second prize), Holland, Italy, and Germany.

CONCLUSION

It is generally agreed that the world press played a very important role in the Second Ecumenical Vatican Council, a role that is all the more impressive for having begun under unfavorable conditions. It is most unusual that world interest should have remained so consistently strong to keep hundreds of journalists from dozens of nations in Rome for the trying sessions each fall from 1962 through 1965. The world news agencies had their regular Roman staffs, and some of the more prominent individual papers sent special correspondents to cover the Council beat. Most of them were edifyingly faithful in their presence at the daily verbal briefings and at the discussions at the Press Panel later in the afternoon.

All of these journalists were genuinely interested in the Council. This explains why they chafed under the restraints imposed in Session I. Restrictions decided upon by higher authority prevented them from telling adequately the story of what their professional sense told them was by general consensus the biggest religious news story of modern times. They felt they had a job to do, wanted to do it well, and felt frustrated at having, so to speak, to work with their hands tied behind their backs.

In the judgment of the author, the performance of the English-language press group, the only one of which he has direct knowledge and experience, was on the whole remarkably creditable. Their efforts to achieve objectivity and accuracy were most praiseworthy. More than one correspondent took the time and trouble to check carefully with his Press Officer, even outside regular working hours, to verify a fact or to confirm an impression.

This does not mean that there were not occasional lapses. With the number and varied backgrounds of individuals it was unavoidable that someone should occasionally go off the deep end. But the author knows of no such case motivated by malicious intent. In most instances, it was a result of using faulty sources, unintentionally misinterpreting proper information or giving it incorrect emphasis. This complaint holds for a good number of headline writers, for whom however the journalists at the Council were not responsible.

It is no exaggeration that the contribution of the press to the Second Vatican Council was invaluable and even indispensable for the proper dissemination of news from the Council Hall. The world assuredly would not have maintained its consistently keen interest over such a protracted period of time had it not been kept carefully informed on a day-to-day basis. This

Conclusion

sums up the essential function of the world press in Vatican II.

We can get a better understanding of this contribution of the press during Vatican II if we compare it with the impressions of the work of the press in the First Vatican Council. Falling back once more on the distinguished Bishop of Birmingham, Doctor Ullathorne, we find him writing in his letter of January 21, 1870, to which we have already referred:

I have never read anything so absurd as the accounts of the Council in the *Times* and other English papers. They don't know what to write and are obliged to invent. Nothing can be more quiet, orderly, and cordial, than the relations of the bishops at all the meetings, and the liberty of speech is perfect, anyone saying just what he pleases on the subjects in question. In fact, unless people in England know things for certain from other sources, they may put down all they read as *lies*. All is going on in perfect order, and the questions before us are being thoroughly discussed.

In a Pastoral Letter to the faithful of his diocese on February 10, 1870, Doctor Ullathorne wrote in greater detail:

Much will you have heard through the newspapers respecting the proceedings of this great Council, and much that is either untrue, or that is the very opposite of the truth, or that is so distorted from the facts, that it no longer has the likeness of truth upon it. . . . Yet, how can it be otherwise? For as to what comes before the Council, and as to what is said in discussion by the members, all who are within the Council are bound to solemn secrecy; whilst outside the Council, the society gathered together from all quarters of the world is a prey to ever-changing rumours, guesses, and imaginations of what is passing within the forbidden doors. About those entrance-doors, and in the great nave of St. Peter's, a gazing crowd, including the correspondents of the newspapers, alive with excited curiosity, and left a prey to their imaginations, get their minds disposed to take fire with fancy at every word they hear dropped, so that out of the smallest materials they build up imaginary scenes and speeches, and fill the minds of the outer world with airy inventions of what is passing within the Council and amongst its members. Thus schemes are said to be under discussion which are not under discussion; designs are attributed to the Council of which the Council knows nothing; and bishops are invested with views and notions and are described as taking this or that course of action, which are utterly unbefitting their characters, and are often in direct opposition to their real sentiments.

Such evaluations of the press as it functioned in the First Vatican Council are in striking contrast with the role of the press in Vatican II.

It can safely be said that both the Vatican and the press gained in the relationships resulting from the recent Council. The Vatican came to have some understanding of the role of world opinion and of the function of the press in keeping this opinion properly enlightened by providing objective news. This new understanding was part of the trend to bring the Roman Catholic Church and the Vatican into closer contact with the world around it. This understanding is still far from perfect, but it would be an error to close one's eyes to the noteworthy progress already achieved.

On the other hand, the press acquired a new understanding and appreciation both of the Vatican as an administrative headquarters and of the Catholic Church and her teaching. Constrained by the demands of their job to acquire some accurate knowledge of the Church's doctrine and discipline in order to write intelligent stories, the representatives of the press acquired either new knowledge or at least new background for knowledge already possessed. The Council provided an opportunity for an invaluable interchange that cannot fail to produce beneficent effects with the passage of time.

Everyone who had any part at all in the evolution of the Second Ecumenical Vatican Council and its presentation to the world regarded himself as singularly privileged to have had a role in this epoch-making event, the effects of which will be felt both inside and outside the Roman Catholic Church for many generations to come. More than one hard-bitten journalist remarked enthusiastically to the English-language Press Officer on the thrill of being so close to the Council and to world history in the making.

These sentiments born of an enthusiastic sense of privilege certainly represent the feelings of the author.

APPENDIX

REPRODUCTION OF ARABIC NEWS BULLETIN

CONCILIO ECUMENICO VATICANO II
Ufficio Stampa

المجمع المسكوني الفاتيكاني الثاني
مكتب الصحافة
القسم العربي
..

روما في ١٦ تشرين اول (اكتوبر) ١٩٦٥

النشرة الرابعة والعشرون

الجلسة العامة الحادية والخمسون بعد المئة

تابع الآباء في جلسة اليوم مناقشة مشروع " خدمة الكهنة وحياتهم " . بدأت الجلسة في تمام الساعة التاسعة بتنصيب الانجيل المقدس الذي قام به سيادة المطران / برتولي ، النائب الرسولي في طرابلس (ليبيا) . وأدار أعمال الجلسة نيافة الكردينال / ليركارو ، رئيس اساقفة بولونيا بايطاليا .

دعا سيادة السكرتير العام الآباء للاشتراك غدا بحفلات تطويب الأب / يعقوب برتييو وهو راهب يسوعي مرسل وشهيد في جزيرة مدغسقر ، وقد عاش من ١٨٣٨ – ١٨٩٦ . وبهذه المناسبة ، قد احتفل بالقداس الالهي هذا الصباح ، قدس الآباتي / أروبي ، الرئيس العام للرهبنة اليسوعية .

تناول الكلام حول مشروع " خدمة الكهنة وحياتهم " كل من :

١)	نيافة الكردينال / ليفيفر	"	رئيس اساقفة بورج (فرنســـــا)
٢)	روجمبـــوا	"	أسقف بروكــــــــا (تنزانيـــــــا)
٣)	روى	"	رئيس اساقفة كيمبك (كنـــدا)
٤)	فلــوريت	"	رئيس اساقفة فلورنسا (ايطاليــا)
٥)	هينــان	"	رئيس اساقفة وستمنستر (انجلتــرا)
٦)	شيــهان	"	رئيس اساقفة بالتيمور (الولايات المتحــدة)
٧)	روســـي	"	رئيس اساقفة ساوباولو (البرازيـــــل) باسم ٤٦ أب برازيلي
٨)	بيـــــا	"	رئيس سكرتارية اتحاد المسيحيين
٩)	سيادة المطران / كلوستر		أسقف سارابايا (اندونســــيا)

105

(١٠)	"	بنك	معاون اسقف جيور (المجر)
(١١)	"	ليفين	معاون أسقف سان أنطونيو (الولايات المتحدة)
(١٢)	"	زيك	أسقف سان بولتن (النمسا)
(١٣)	"	فرنند ز/كونتى	أسقف كوردوبا (اسبانيا)
(١٤)	"	باريلا	أسقف شيستوكوا (بولندا)
(١٥)	"	سوارس	أسقف بيرا (موزمبيق)
(١٦)	"	اند جمو	أسقف انكونجزابا (الكامرون)

١) المشروع الحالى مرض واللجنة التى أعدته تستحق الثناء ، ولكن لمن المؤسف أنه عند عرضه وذلائف الكاهن يهمل أبوته الروحية . يصف مختلف أنواع الخدمة الكهنوتية دون أن يبين ما هو الهدف الموجهة نحوه وغاية الكهنوت هى تشييد جسد المسيح . تلك هى المهمة الأساسية ، الخاصة بالكاهن . وتسمو خدمته فى الابوة الروحية التى يولد بفعلها أعضاء جدد فى جسد المسيح بواسطة الكنيسة وفى الكنيسة حسب تعبير القديس بولس . ومهام التعليم والادارة والتقديس هى أنواع من ممارسة هذه الابوة التى تنير هدف الخدمة الكهنوتية وشرتها وعظمتها . فيجب التعبير عن ذلك

REPRODUCTION OF CHINESE NEWS BULLETIN

CONCILIO ECUMENICO VATICANO II
Ufficio Stampa

CONCILIO ECUMENICO VATICANO II
Ufficio Stampa

September 30, 1963

NEWS BULLETIN NO. 1*
GENERAL CONGREGATION NO. 37

The opening mass was celebrated by Archbishop Giovanni Colombo, successor of Pope Paul VI in Milan. The mass was celebrated in the Ambrosian rite, with the entire assembly joining in the prayers and responses. After the mass the Gospel Book was enthroned by Archbishop Felici, the Secretary General of the Council. The session was presided over by Cardinal Agagianian, Prefect of the Congregation for the Propagation of the Faith, acting for the first time as one of the four Moderators appointed by the Holy Father.

Before the discussion on business the Secretary General proposed the transmission of the following message to the Holy Father in the name of the Council Members:

"At the opening of this General Congregation may we be permitted to express our sentiments of filial devotion to him who in the first session of this Council

---

* Text of the first bulletin of Session II, prepared according to policy prevailing in Session I.

This and the following bulletin are the verbatim English translations (no editorial changes made) provided the newsmen accredited to the Council.

shared in our Council work and was then taken from among us by the Holy Spirit and elected to the Supreme Ministry of the Catholic Church.

"Most Holy Father, last year your words were directed us as a brother. Yesterday the heart of a father opened up to us. May Your Holiness now deign to accept our most lively and joyful thanks for having wished to point out and to fervently recommend the course to be followed in our work. Through our prayers and our work we hope and work together with your Holiness that the Holy Catholic Church may appear before the entire world as the mystery of Christ and as the life of Christ Himself on earth."

Today's discussions stressed the point, that as it stands, the schema is a satisfactory foundation for fruitful Council discussion, intended to provide a broader and clearer vision of the Church. It was observed, however, that it has some weaknesses which can lead to misunderstandings as also some obscure points likely to give rise to doubt and uncertainty. It was also requested that more space should be given in the schema to the Blessed Mother, even though there will later be a complete schema dedicated to Mary as Mother of God and Mother of the Church.

A change in the present title of the schema was requested in order to have it read, "The Church of Christ." The observation was made that presenting the Church as a "mystery" at the very outset of the schema makes it difficult for the people to understand, because they have vague ideas as to the nature of a mystery.

Lastly, the schema expresses the long-awaited declaration of the sacramental nature of the episcopal consecration. This point, however, needs further clarification and must also be assigned a theological note.

The schema emphasizes the continuity of the Councils, answers the need for a more complete and clearer presentation of the doctrine of the Mystical Body, and offers a solid foundation of the ecumenical movement. Nevertheless, it was observed, it insists unduly on the equality of the members of the Church without stressing sufficiently the exercise of authority. It is necessary, likewise, to avoid any possible confusion on the problem of the "universal priesthood" of the people of God. It is likewise necessary to have a clearer, better, and more profound formulation of the apostolate of the laity.

Although it is regarded as substantially positive the schema does not offer any adequate presentation of the Church for non-Christians, with the result that the Church remains for them almost unintelligible. This defect becomes all the more grave because the vast majority of the human race is made up of non-Christians, to whom the Church has the task of announcing the message of the Gospel.

A proposal was made that the general structure of the schema should be re-worked in such a way as to make more natural the transition from the concept of the Church as the Mystical Body to that of the people of God, and from the equality of its members to that of the hierarchical order, as well as from the bishops to priests and deacons. A desire was also expressed to eliminate from the schema juridical concepts, exhortations and the repeated explanations of the primacy of the sovereign Pontiff.

It was stressed that the Church derives from the Cross, and that this fact should be reflected also in her external life and in her apostolate. Greater emphasis should likewise be given to the theological foundation for the apostolate of the laity.

A request was made for a clarification of certain particular aspects of the schema. The Church, it was said, exists from the beginning of the world and consequently the Church of the Old Testament is not merely a pre-figuration but a true and a perfect society.

A strong recommendation was made that the heads of non-Christian religions be invited to the Council as observers. Satisfaction was expressed that the doctrine on the Church is formulated in the schema with clarity, concern for pastoral and ecumenical consideration, without the cold rigidity of juridical style and with an abundance of citations from scripture.

It was announced that tomorrow on the conclusion of the discussion on the schema in general, a vote of the Fathers will be taken on its approval in principle.

. . . .

At the beginning of the session the Secretary General explained the various modifications introduced into the rules and procedure of the Council which were already made known in the letter of the Holy Father to the Dean of the Sacred College on September 14. The five Under-Secretaries read in their respective languages—Arabic, English, French, German, and Spanish—various announcements. The Council Fathers wishing to speak during the General Congregations are requested to notify the Secretary General at least three days in advance and to present either a summary of, still better, the complete text of what they wish to say. The time limit for individual speakers is still 10 minutes, but 2 minutes before the end of this period the telephone near the speaker's microphone will ring to warn him that his time is running out so that he may bring his remarks to a close.

The obligation of secrecy extends to anything connected with the schemas to be discussed and the work of the individual commissions. The greater prudence and moderation are recommended to all the Fathers in all circumstances for anything connected with the work taking place in the Council hall.

It was likewise announced that there will be no further appointments of Council experts since the number of those already designated is quite sufficient to meet the needs of the Council.

After the reading of these announcements the Cardinal Agagianian took the floor to welcome the Council Fathers, particularly those taking part in the Council for the first time, such as the Prefects Apostolic and the lay observers. His Eminence, in conclusion invited all those present to resume the work of the Council under the guidance of Paul VI drawing their inspiration from the policy discourse pronounced by His Holiness yesterday in the Vatican Council.

For the first part of the schema, including the title, the introduction, and the first two chapters, 372 amendments had been proposed, one dealing with the title, nine for the introduction, 156 for the first chapter and 206 for the second chapter.

The following speakers addressed the assembly on the schema in general: Cardinal Joseph Frings, Archbishops of Cologne, Germany, speaking for 65 German and Scandinavian-speaking Council Fathers; Cardinal Joseph Siri, Archbishop of Genoa; His Beatitude Ignatius Peter Batanian, Patriarch of Cilicia of the Armenians in Lebanon; Archbishop Casimir Morcillo, Archbishop of Saragossa, Spain; Archbishop Carlo A. Ferrero di Cavallerleone, Titular Archbishop of Trebisondo; Archbishop Peter Ngo-Din-Thuc, Archbishop of Hué, Vietnam; Bishop Giuseppe Gargitter, Bishop of Bressanone, Italy; Archbishop Erminegildo Florit, Archbishop of Florence, Italy.

At today's meeting 2258 Council Fathers were present; other Council members arrived later, coming from their respective Sees.

The assembly adjourned at 12:15 after the recitation of the usual prayers.

CONCILIO ECUMENICO VATICANO II
Ufficio Stampa

October 1, 1963

NEWS BULLETIN NO. 2*
GENERAL CONGREGATION NO. 38

The Mass was celebrated by the Most Reverend John Charles McGuaid, Archbishop of Dublin. The Gospel Book was enthroned by Archbishop Philip Nabaa, Melchite Archbishop of Beirut, Under-Secretary of the Council. The work of the meeting was directed by Cardinal Giacomo Lercaro, Archbishop of Bologna, one of the four Moderators.

At the beginning of the session the General Secretary read to the assembly from the Apostolic Administrator of Mazara del Vallo, in Sicily announcing the grave illness of the Archbishop of that Diocese, Archbishop Joachim Di Lee and informing the Council that the Archbishop was offering his sufferings for the happy continuance of the Council work. Later in the session, the General Secretary likewise announced that Archbishop Thomas Pothacamury, of Bangalore, India, was also at the point of death. In the name of the assembly the General Secretary sent assurances to both of the prayers of the Council in their hour of trial.

* Text of second bulletin of Session II, prepared according to the new press policy approved by Pope Paul VI.

The following Council Fathers took part in the morning's discussion, either by addressing the Fathers or presenting their remarks in writing:

1. Cardinal Raul Silva Henriquez, Archbishop of Santiago, Chile, in the name of 44 Latin-American Bishops;
2. Cardinal Laurean Rugambwa, Bishop of Bukoba in Tangyanika, in the name of numerous Bishops from Africa and Madagascar;
3. Archbishop Maximus Hérmaniuk, Archbishop of Winnipeg, for the Ukranians in Canada;
4. Archbishop Gabriel Garrone, Archbishop of Toulouse, France;
5. Bishop Primo Gasbarri, Auxiliary Bishop of Velletri in Italy;
6. Bishop Arthur Elchinger, Coadjutor Bishop of Strasbourg, France;
7. Archbishop Armando Fares Archbishop of Catanzaro, Italy;
8. Archbishop Adrian Djajasepoetra, Archbishop of Djakarta, Indonesia, in the name of 31 Indonesian bishops;
9. Bishop Sergio Mendez Arceo, Bishop of Cuernavaca, Mexico;
10. Bishop Giocondo Grotti, Prelate of Acre and Purus, Brazil;
11. Bishop Joseph Guffens, Titular Bishop of Germaniciana;
12. Bishop Jose Pont y Gol, Bishop of Segorbe-Castellon, Spain.

Later in the discussion Cardinal Ernesto Ruffini, Archbishop of Palermo, Italy, spoke on the introduction and the first chapter of the Schema.

The meeting was attended by 2,301 Council Fathers.

Comments from the speakers on the schema on the Church in general can be reduced to the following:

1. The schema is quite acceptable as a working basis for further study and discussion. Chapter 3 should be divided into two chapters, one of which would treat of "the people of God" while the second would treat of "the laity." The first of these chapters should stress the ideas of "prophetic people," "priestly people," "royal people." This chapter should have second place in the schema before the one which treats of the hierarchy. There should also be a treatment of the Church finding its perfection in the saints and also a treatment of the Blessed Virgin Mary, but without a separate schema.

2. The schema provides a broader vision of the Church and studies effectively its internal and external aspects. The point should be stressed that the missionary function of the Church is the same as that of the Incarnate Work; the evangelization of the world. Reference is made to missionary work but the text is silent regarding this evangelization which is the essential function of the Church. The task of the Church is the same as that received by the Son from the Father. The schema seems to suppose that the Church is already a completed reality, whereas it is still in the process of organization and development. Consequently, there is not enough emphasis on the missionary aspects of the

Church. Not with reference to the missionary apostolate in the ordinary sense of the word, but to the mission of the universal Church. The Church today is present everywhere in the world and is a missionary Church even where the faithful are in the majority. Hence the Church must regard herself as "missionary" always and everywhere. Lastly, the text should contain a clearer treatment of "the people of God."

3. The schema is quite acceptable because of its scriptural content, its frequent use of the traditions of the Oriental Churches, as evidenced in numerous citations from the Church Fathers of the East. The schema is also acceptable because of its formal insistence on the collegiate of the episcopate and because of its ecumenical spirit. The text is silent however, on the authority of the College of Bishops over the universal Church. Mere concern for the interest of the Church at large is not sufficient. This two-fold power, mainly that of the Roman Pontiff and that of the College of Bishops should find expression in the constitution of a kind of "apostolic college." This college would be presided over by the Pope, and its members would be patriarchs, Cardinals at the head of diocese, and other Archbishops and Bishops, to be chosen according to the norms of the set-up at the proper time. It would have two secretariats, the first for the Oriental Churches and the second for the Latin Churches. The foundation for this, "apostolic college" would be in the words of Christ, handing over jurisdiction to Peter and his successors as well as to the other apostles and their successors.

Such a college would emphasize the fact that the universal jurisdiction of Bishops is not restricted to the time of ecumenical councils. The schema presents an idea of the Church which is too abstract and unrealistic. It would be desirable to state clearly that the union of Christians in the Holy Spirit does not destroy the union which exists in the natural order, for example in families, cities, and nations. The Church is not a kind of super-state aiming to absorb such natural unions. The text makes too frequent use of the expression "the College of Bishops with its head the Roman Pontiff." The schema should provide a clear definition of the college of bishops, showing that it embraces the entire episcopate with the Roman Pontiff. Lastly, there is undue insistence of the "Roman" aspects of the Church.

4. The schema needs to be completed and perfected. The treatment of the Blessed Virgin Mary should be transferred to this schema on the Church in order to make for better balance. Greater emphasis should be put on the riches contained in the idea and image of the kingdom of God. The text gives us an excessive static idea of the Church and does not insist sufficiently on its missionary character in expectation of the kingdom of God. There should be a treatment of tradition, showing how tradition assists the Church in the solution of not a few problems arising from research concerning revelation.

5. The present schema reflects greater organic unity than the previous text, and is more astral in tone as well as more biblical and more patristic. The chapter on the relationships and the civil governments has been

omitted but a thorough treatment of this question would be useful not only from the juridical but also from the pastoral viewpoint, as well for countries where the Church is respected as for those in which she is persecuted.

6. The schema answers a crying catechetical need by presenting in greater unity the various aspects and figures of the Church. There should be an introduction on the word of God founding and actively assembling the Church. This subject should be treated here, not in the discussion of revelation and tradition. Tradition should be regarded as a living and life-giving reality. We should consider the people of God as being actively ruled by the word of God and the Church as serving the faithful as custodian and witness of this same word of God. This would bring into bolder relief the essentially dynamic aspect of tradition. The treatment of the vocation to sanctity should have a more eschatological orientation to serve as a basis for Christian hope in a nihilistic and materialistic age. In the center of this eschatological consideration there is the recapitulation of all creation in Christ. This is the fulfillment of the entire economy of salvation. In those considerations the Blessed Virgin is not given her proper place. This place cannot be understood except in reference to the mystery of the Church. Treating of the Blessed Virgin in the schema of the Church, rather than in a schema apart, does not detract in any way from her dignity.

7. The text of the schema could remain unchanged but each chapter should be preceded by a brief intro-

duction explaining the points to be set forth. There would be question of a synthetic explanation which would be adapted to the present day mentality, the substance, the scope, the meaning, and inter-unity of the doctrine subsequently formulated.

8. As has already been suggested, it should be pointed out that the Church is speaking in obedience to God and not merely as a strictly human institution. For this reason the schema should also make mention of the liturgy which is a duty of the entire people of God to which the Church, acting always as a missionary, must not only bring light, but also teach how to pray.

9. Basically, the schema is acceptable. An indespensable condition for the success of any apostolate is confidence in one's fellow men. We might raise the question whether those in positions of authority, clerics not excepted, have learned from the experience of these last few years to have this confidence.

10. As regards the formulation of the text, attention was called to the fact that its explanations lack clarity, contain many repetitions and too many quotations. Consequently it will be necessary to give the text greater unity and clearer coordination.

At the conclusion of this debate, Cardinal Michael Browne assured the assembly that all the suggestions presented on the schema in general assembly would be given all due consideration by the competent commission.

While the Council Fathers were preparing to cast their votes on the general presentation of the schema, the Secretary General announced that the schemata to be discussed later would be as follows: The Blessed Virgin Mary as Mother of the Church, Bishops and the governments of dioceses, the Apostolate of the Laity, and Ecumenism.

The results of the voting were as follows: Fathers present, 2,301; Favorable votes, 2,231; Unfavorable votes, 43; Favorable votes with reservations, 3; Null and void votes, 24.

After the favorable vote on the schema in general, discussion was opened on the first chapter. Different formulas and expressions found in this chapter were criticized both from the exegetical and theological viewpoints. The first chapter should discuss particularly the principle of Christian unity, namely of the Eucharist which is the center and foundation of unity, thus emphasizing the relationship existing between the Eucharist and the Church.

The meeting adjourned at 12:15.

ADDRESS OF POPE PAUL VI
TO COUNCIL PRESS CORPS

November 26, 1965

WE CAN sincerely say that it is a great pleasure to be here with you today in the place where you work. Even if things are never as perfect as one would like them to be, you can at least feel when you make use of the faculties at your disposal that the Church takes an interest in your work and does her best to help you to carry out your professional engagements.

One cannot but be impressed by the tremendous efforts which you have made and the work you have had to do, often in circumstances which demand that action be taken very quickly because of modern laws of communications. One is struck too by the considerable importance of the role you have played since the beginning of this Second Vatican Ecumenical Council.

If the Church has felt, as never before in her 2,000-year history, that many millions of men were taking an interest in the reunion of bishops from all over the world, this, gentlemen, is undoubtedly owed very largely to you.

We congratulate you and thank you with all Our heart!

On the other hand, We like to think that the gain has not been one-sided and that you too have profited greatly from the possibility offered to you of being able to observe the life of the supreme organ of the Church from very close at hand. Your interest in the Council itself and in all the happenings, great and small, which have marked its progress, shows that you have been aware of the problems that have arisen and that you have understood their importance for men of today—the immense mass of your readers and listeners.

While progressively discovering the dimensions of the conciliar event, you have at the same time acquired a better understanding of just how profoundly important the questions confronting the Council are for religious thought and for all of mankind. You have learned something of the relationship between the doctrine of the Church and the life of man: his history, civilization, and destiny.

You have realized the Church's vitality and her effort to remain faithful to her origins and her aims, to her traditions and to the new needs of society, both civil and ecclesiastical, and you have discovered what was the profound meaning of the *aggiornamento* which Pope John XXIII, Our venerated predecessor, felt was needed, and to which you have contributed so much in making it understood by the general public.

In making this effort of progressive discovery, you will have doubtless experienced how difficult it is really to understand the Council. Because although it is relatively simple to describe the exterior phenomena which characterize it, it is surely much more difficult to lead minds into its doctrinal and spiritual interior. Without doubt many purely superficial accounts, unfounded and misleading hypotheses, and marginal interpretations which fail to capture the meaning of events must be attributed to this very real difficulty.

Thus it is, for example, that concepts and categories in use in lay society are too often imposed on the happenings of the Council without discernment in order to dramatize description by use of current terminology.

Who among you does not see a pressing invitation arise from this very difficulty? In order to inform one must be informed; in order to teach one must know; in order to carry out your very worthy task as informants you must have understood.

So it is that the Church must be known before she can be spoken about: she must be studied before she can be known. In order to lead it is necessary to understand oneself. This is not easy, because the real life of the Church is completely interior and spiritual, and it is only at this level that one is able to perceive it, to appreciate its true value, and to enjoy, if one can, its magnificent and mysterious experiences.

The function of information, the press, radio, and television—in a word, of all the audiovisual techniques —is truly considerable.

This importance is growing all the time, and with it, gentlemen, the gravity of your duties. It depends ever more on you, in so far as a ceaselessly growing part of humanity is concerned, if the men and women of today have access to the truth. This means that, guided by a desire to do good and a respect for moral and spiritual values, you can accomplish a mission that we do not hesitate to describe as providential.

You can image that, for our part, we are convinced of the value of your mission; we have a great desire to do all in our power to help you accomplish it ever more effectively, taking into account the imperative needs of your professional obligations.

As We have said at the beginning of this informal encounter, We wanted, for the entire duration of the Council, to satisfy as far as possible your legitimate request to receive news and information from a reliable source. With this aim in mind, the Council press office was formed, and We are happy to have this occasion to pay public tribute to those in charge for their daily toil, often obscure and austere, in your service and the service of truth.

You will say to Us: "And now?"—now that the Council is coming to an end. Certainly the life of the Church will continue both in its visible center and throughout the nations of the entire world. We know that a great effort has been made by several of the episcopal conferences to help all the religious informants to fulfill their duties, by communicating information to them and also by furnishing them with indications and explanations which are often necessary to give an account of the life of such a complex organism. We are very happy about this, and We congratulate both promoters and directors from the bottom of our heart.

You may also ask about the Holy See. Well, you must know, the Holy See is completely disposed to continue this service, as far as is possible, so that news is transmitted to you with the rapidity and fulness required by the needs of today and the importance of information.

We wish to add something which will hardly surprise you—you who over the years have become "habitues," intimates, one might say, of Vatican surroundings.

There is no need to explain to you that the Holy See is a very special organism by reason of its origin, its nature, and its aims. By this We mean that this special world has, naturally, its special methods, particularly with regard to its manner of diffusing information. The Vatican is anxious to do so, and in time surely, but without ever succumbing to that fever and passion which are sometimes characteristic of reporters in the exercise of their profession. There is no need to repeat that sensation and spectacle are not waiting for you here but, on the contrary, objectivity and serenity.

You know well that if sometimes the Holy See seems reserved when giving news, it is not in order to shirk what has become an obligation in the modern world. In fact, an organism which you know works toward this end, the press service of *Osservatore Romano,* in spite of the feeble means at its disposal has already rendered great service to many among you and, without doubt, will continue to do so in the future. The reserve of the Holy See is due to something else: it is the fear, unhappily well founded, of being misinterpreted.

Because, too often still—no one can deny it—Vatican news is diffused in such a way as to consider the respect due to persons, and care for the truth, far from basic.

By this We mean, gentlemen, that improvement of

this situation must be brought about by you too.

For Our part We are desirous to help you in the service of truth, but in this service only and not in other interests to which the truth may be alien. The more journalists are straightforward and upright in the performance of their duties, the more they will find the attention which they legitimately expect and the objective information which they need from the competent Vatican organs.

It is, therefore, a brotherly exchange, both prudent and sincere, which should be ever more firmly established, and a mutual help which should continue to develop itself. Thus, without doubt, each will profit, both sides will be mutually satisfied, above all the truth will be better served, and men will be able to know her better: this truth which for Christians bears the name of love and the face of Christ the Redeemer, whose humble vicar We are.

Gentlemen, We should like to continue this conversation. At least We should like to finish by extending Our thanks to each and every one of you for the good work done, and by wishing that you will leave Rome with happy memories, the joy of a more profound discovery of the Church and of the Holy See, and by vowing that we will meet again. After the Council, your work—as Ours—continues, and Ours will undoubtedly contribute to support yours!

May God bless your persons, all who are dear to you, and all that you do in the service of truth.

ADDRESS OF POPE JOHN XXIII
TO COUNCIL PRESS CORPS

October 13, 1962

THE PURPOSE of today's audience is to express the esteem We have for the representatives of the press and the importance We attribute to your profession.

On the day after Our election, We arranged to meet a special group of journalists from all over the world. In the succeeding four years of Our pontifical service, We have had several opportunities of addressing words of encouragement and exhortation to members of your profession.

For the purposes of the Council We have opened, as you know, a press office and a secretariat for the different forms of communication. We have set up also a commission in the Council to devote itself to the lay apostolate and to the apostolates of the press, radio, and entertainment. This will show you the importance your vocation has had for Us and, at the same time, Our desire to help you to carry it out well.

The solemn occasion of the opening of this twenty-first ecumenical council of the Catholic Church prompted Us to give you a special mark of Our good will. We also felt keenly that We must tell you personally how much We desire your loyal cooperation in presenting this great event to the public in its true colors.

We have, of set purpose, chosen the Sistine Chapel to be the setting of this audience in order to manifest its importance. At the foot of Michelangelo's famous fresco of the Last Judgment—as We said yesterday to the special missions—each one can reflect with profit on his responsibilities. Yours, gentlemen, are great. You are at the service of truth and you come up to men's expectations in so far as you serve it faithfully.

We speak purposely of the expectations of men—of men, that is, in general—for though the press may have at one time reached no more than a select few, it is obvious that today it directs the thoughts and feelings and emotions of a great part of mankind. For this reason, the distortion of truth by the organs of information can have incalculable consequences.

There is admittedly a great temptation to pander to the taste of a particular section, to be more concerned with speed than accuracy, to be more interested in the "sensational" than in the objective truth. And so undue prominence is given to some incidental detail, and the reality is softpedaled in the way an event is presented or a situation or an opinion or a belief is summed up.

That, of course, is a way of obscuring the truth, and, if it is serious in any context, how much more so is it when it is a question of the most intimate and sacred matter of religion and the soul's relationship with God!

An ecumenical council has naturally external and secondary aspects, which can easily be used to satisfy the curiosity of an importunate public.

It can also, in the long run, exert a happy influence on the relations between men in the social, and even in the political, sphere.

But it is essentially a great religious event, and it is Our earnest desire that you should help to make this fact well known. This will show you what tact and discretion, what care for understanding and accuracy, one may rightly expect here of a reporter with the honor of his noble profession at heart.

We ask of all of you an effort to understand and to make others understand that these solemn conciliar sessions are primarily religious and spiritual.

By means of the conscientious fulfillment of your mission as reporters of the Council, We look forward, gentlemen, to very happy results as regards the attitude of world opinion toward the Catholic Church in general, her institutions, and her teachings.

Deep-rooted prejudices can exist on this subject in different areas, in particular where people do not enjoy faithful and objective reporting. These serve to keep alive in men's hearts pockets of resistance, of suspicion, and of misunderstanding, the consequences of which are regrettable for the advancement of harmony between men and nations.

These prejudices rest most often on inaccurate or incomplete information. People attribute to the Church doctrines which she does not profess, people blame her for attitudes which she has taken in definite historical circumstances, and they unjustifiably generalize those attitudes without taking into account their accidental and particular character.

What occasion could be more fitting, gentlemen, than an ecumenical council to establish true contact with the life of the Church and to gain information from responsible sources which clearly reflect the thought of the episcopacy and of the universal Church here assembled! The mere announcement of the Council has aroused in the whole world a remarkable interest to which you have largely contributed.

And even yesterday—We must congratulate you for this—it was thanks to your presence and to your often difficult work that, for the first time in history, the entire world was enabled to take part in the opening of an ecumenical council, directly by radio and television, and also by the press reports. It is Our earnest desire that your accounts should arouse the friendly interest of the public in the Council and help eventually to correct mistaken or incomplete views of it.

You could make it known that there are no political machinations afoot. You will be able to see and to report the true motives which inspire the Church's action in the world, and bear witness to the fact that she has nothing to hide, that she follows a straight path without any deviations and that she wants nothing so much as the truth, for men's happiness, and for a fruitful concord among the nations of every continent.

And so, thanks to you, many prejudices can be dissipated. In serving the truth you will at the same time have assisted that "interior disarmament" which is the absolutely necessary condition for the establishment of true peace on this earth.

These, gentlemen, are Our hopes, Our incentives, and Our desires. Permit Us to add a word of gratitude. For We appreciate your efforts to inform the public of the manifestation of the Church's life, and We have, on our own account, good reason for satisfaction in the respectful understanding with which you have, in general, spoken of Our own humble person.

Called by the designs of Providence to this high office, and that at an advanced age, after many and varied experiences, We find, certainly, comfort and encouragement in what is said about Us: Our personality, character, apostolic enterprises, but none of that disturbs the tranquil peace of Our soul. In 1953, when We took leave of France, which has ever remained dear to Us, We said:

"For my personal consolation so long as I shall live —and wherever it may please the Holy Father to appoint me to a work and a responsibility in the service of the Church—I ask no more than that each good Frenchman, recalling my humble name and my stay amongst you, may be able to say: he was a loyal and a peaceable priest, always and on every occasion a true and sincere friend of France."

We repeat today, gentlemen, that wish of ten years

ago, and We extend it in applying it to your profession. We ask no more than that you may always and on every occasion be able to write down as Our single and true title of honor: he was a priest before God and before the people, a true and sincere friend of all nations.

And now, We will give you Our blessing. In the words of the beautiful biblical expression which is perhaps known to you, "a father's blessing is the buttress of his children's house" (Eccl. 3, 11). That is a thought that is familiar to Us, one which an old father may permit himself when he looks with tenderness on his sons.

It is accordingly from an affectionate heart that We call down upon you, in conclusion, the best graces from on high, and We bestow upon you, and upon your families and all those who are dear to you, the apostolic blessing.